The author and two friends—July 1965

Raccoons
Are the Brightest People

by STERLING NORTH

ILLUSTRATED WITH PHOTOGRAPHS

AN AVON BOOK

AVON BOOKS
A division of
The Hearst Corporation
959 Eighth Avenue
New York, New York 10019

First Avon Printing, August, 1967

Cover photo by Ed Park—Three Lions

To the one girl and the many raccoons in my life

The photographs illustrating
this book were taken by many
photographers, including:

Leonard Lee Rue
Wallace Kirkland
Jessie Smith
Sterling North
Clarence E. Olson
Reed I. MacDonald
Glenn Zahn
Arthur Witman
Harry C. James
F. W. Stuewer
W. J. Collings, Jr.
and others.

For more detailed and specific
acknowledgments please see pages 189-192.

Contents

	In Answer to Many Letters	13
ONE	A Place Fit for Raccoons	15
TWO	Flora's First Year	45
THREE	The Raccoons Who Came to Dinner	79
FOUR	Raccoons as Pets	107
FIVE	St. Francis of Northernaire	136
SIX	Long Live the Wilderness	176

Raccoons Are the Brightest People

In Answer to Many Letters

How do you attract creatures from the woods?

Do raccoons make good pets, or was Rascal an exception?

Do wild animals get along well together?

I think *raccoons are the brightest people*. Will you please write another book about them?

Did you ever see Rascal again?

Did you keep your boyhood promise never to shoot or trap any bird or animal?

Every day for the last three years the large mailbox we have installed at the foot of our drive has been crammed with letters from readers ranging in age from nine to ninety and postmarked from every state in the Union and from fourteen other countries where *Rascal* has been published.

This new book is a partial reply to the intelligent, sensitive and sometimes profound questions asked by more than sixteen thousand correspondents. It is an attempt to repay in kind the children and adults of this world who have sent me wood carvings, water colors, crayon drawings and letters in honor of the little raccoon who was my best friend and constant companion during my somewhat lonesome childhood.

The last two queries listed above were also the most frequent. I can answer both immediately. No, alas, I never saw Rascal again, although we have friendly raccoons at the back door every evening. Yes, I did keep the promise I made at the age of twelve. Never again did I shoot or trap any bird or animal (with the single exception of a few snapping turtles, so dangerous to our newly hatched mallards and wood ducklings).

On the following pages I will try to answer some of those other pertinent questions concerning myself, my family and our enchanted valley.

Sterling North
Morristown, New Jersey

August 1966

ONE

A Place Fit for Raccoons

It seemed we had been searching all our married life for "a place fit for raccoons"—that is, a rural refuge with clean, running water and big trees. Gladys and the children may have felt this urge less keenly than I did, since they had never owned a pet raccoon and had seen very few in the wild. But they knew how passionately I felt about raccoons and all other wilderness creatures—in fact, about conservation in general. The stories I had told them about my boyhood in Wisconsin had excited their imagination.

On this evening in June 1943 we were moving from the Midwest to the Eastern Seaboard, and at the moment were traveling northward on the historic highway which leads from Princeton, New Jersey to Morristown. We paused on a bridge where the ancient trail crosses a cold, clear brook named for an early settler named Primrose. It was from this pure stream that Washington's troops obtained their drinking water during the bitter winter of 1779–80, a winter far more severe than that at Valley Forge.

The moon was enmeshed in the boughs arching over us. There was the music of falling water and a path of moonlight on a little lake above the dam. Suddenly the silent valley was pierced by an insistent trill. We had thought that our eleven-year-old daughter and fourteen-year-old son were asleep on the back seat. But now we heard Arielle whisper to David:

"Listen! a screech owl!"

"Not exactly a screech owl," David said sleepily.

"You're right, son. It's a family of raccoons."

"But they do trill like little owls," Arielle insisted.

A moment later the darkness was split by a spine-chilling scream.

"Merciful heavens!" my wife asked. "What was that?"

"The same raccoons," I said with elation. "They've met competition in their hunt for crayfish."

"But won't they tear each other to pieces?"

"Very unlikely. They mostly bluff."

In fact there had been no fight, if I had judged correctly. There were a few mild growls. Then the churring and purring of the original raccoons commenced once again, while from farther up the stream came a similar contented harmonizing from the intrusive family, now hunting their crayfish and minnows in safer waters.

Raccoons are among the most highly articulate of all wild animals. The gorilla is credited with a vocabulary of twenty-two sounds and the chimpanzee twenty-three. From my experience I would say that raccoons utter thirteen or fourteen calls and many nuances of each. There are tender little tremolos of various pitches which are almost songs, many meaningful notes of warning and the continuous family conversation which helps to keep the mother and her tribe together on their nightly foraging trips.

A place fit for raccoons? To ardent conservationists such as we, this also means a place fit for human beings!

So much of our continent has been ripped and ravaged by heedless and greedy men, so many forests slaughtered, so many acres deprived of native grasses which once protected them from erosion! In my childhood many American streams were still unpolluted, but by 1943 hundreds of lakes and rivers had become unfit for man or raccoon. Wetlands, of utmost importance to the conservation of water and wild life, were already crisscrossed with ugly drainage ditches. The lethal hand of "progress" had paved, with asphalt and cement, areas where the deer once grazed and the violets and anemones carpeted the meadows and oak openings.

We had searched the entire region around Chicago without finding a single tract of virgin forest. Was it possible that we had discovered such an Eden by moonlight on our first evening in the East?

I switched on the car lights, and there, in reflected radiance, were five pairs of green-gold eyes—those of the mother raccoon and her four kits. We found a nearby motel and slept more serenely than we had in many weeks. It was cool and fresh that evening with a breeze through the big trees. And more than once during the night we heard the churring of raccoons, the sharp, high bark of a fox and the plaintive call of the whippoorwill.

We felt when we awoke that what we had seen the night before must have been a dream. How could a valley which had been inhabited for nearly three hundred years be as unchanged and unspoiled as it had seemed by moonlight? Retracing our route to the bridge, then curving up a road once used by the colonial troops, we found that we had not been mistaken. A few widely scattered and handsome old houses, each surrounded by many wooded acres, nestled comfortably between the hills adjoining the heavily forested national park. And on the wide green lawn of one of the most gracious of these homes we saw a small sign saying "For Sale."

Gladys, whom I married for more romantic reasons, has a sense of orderliness. Her checkbook balances. She keeps our library of ten thousand books alphabetically arranged in twenty categories. Nor did she fail us now.

For many weeks she had been clipping real estate ads from the *New York Times,* pasting them on cards, and arranging them by region. We had seen and rejected an old stone house overlooking the battlefield at Princeton. We had not searched Long Island nor nearby Connecticut. Perhaps we had reached our goal. So now my wife flipped through the file to Morristown, New Jersey. There it was, the very house we were viewing:

PERFECT FOR WRITER OR ARTIST. Thirteen-room colonial which reputedly once housed Mad Anthony Wayne. Valley much the same as it was three centuries ago. Two acre lake with swans. Deer, wild ducks, egrets and herons. New barn with drinking cups in each box stall. Twenty-seven wooded acres, riding trails, two trout streams, adjoining national park. Tastefully remodeled. Many bathrooms and fireplaces. Serenity and charming neighbors!

What lyricists these ad writers are! But this one seemed to be telling the truth. There were indeed swans on the little lake, two sparkling streams and a barn and house which were more than presentable. All up the valley and covering the side of Tea Mountain were ancient trees, lush and green.

We tried three doors, but all were locked.

"The house doesn't matter too much," Arielle said. "Look at that barn! Perfect for our horse and Jersey heifers."

"And the lake to swim in," David added.

I could see that we wouldn't have insurmountable difficulties persuading the children.

Our enthusiasm mounted as we strolled down a blue-stoned riding trail into the deep shade of tall white oaks, beeches, maples and tulip trees. In the hush, Gladys murmured, "Our own Green Mansions." We have not read W. H. Hudson for many years, but as we remember the best of his books, they express the magic of that first walk in our valley. Across the bridge below the upper waterfall, thrushes were singing from groves of blossoming rhododendrons.

An island in the creek seemed to be composed of unglaciated sand, tiny quartz crystals nearly as sharp as the day they cooled from the molten rock, pink feldspar and flakes of shining mica. Perhaps the miniature mountain on this property had deflected the last advance of the glacier, sending the ice down adjoining valleys. Pointed and precise as the minute quartz pebbles themselves were the signatures of deer and raccoons and sandpipers imprinted on the island. A muskrat had opened a small fresh-water clam on the previous evening. His webbed hind feet, and trailing tail, had recorded the story.

We had seldom seen larger oaks or beeches. Some of them took two of us to reach around. In a later year when several of these forest giants were felled by a hurricane we counted the annual rings on the saw cuts and discovered that a score were more than two hundred years old.

Returning along the trail to investigate the barn we found an empty haymow with a floor smooth enough for dancing, a room with archery targets, box stalls for horses and calving cows, and three stanchions which would exactly accommodate Diana, Phoebe and Aphrodite. Gladys had become entranced with mythology at an early age, and every Jersey we had ever owned had been christened with a pagan and poetic name. Several proved to be as wild as any reveler on Mount Olympus.

That we were obsessed with the idea of owning a farm was not surprising. I was born in southern Wisconsin on the shores of Lake Koshkonong with its flocks of wild geese and ducks and its limitless supply of black bass, pickerel and wall-eyed pike. All along that lake and nearby streams and rivers large herds of dairy cows grazed in well-watered pastures. Farm houses of brick, native limestone or neat white clapboard surmounted almost every shaded hill, surrounded by other buildings, usually dominated by a large red dairy barn and white silo.

Tractors and other sophisticated agricultural machines were only beginning to encroach on the old-fashioned plows and harrows of the horse-drawn era. Farm work was hard but rewarding. I doubt if ever before, or since, mankind has had such a sense of security. My great-grandfather and grandfather had come from England in the 1840's and had carved from the Wisconsin wilderness a large homestead. The fourteen-room brick house had all the comforts of those primitive days, and the surrounding acres were green with corn, clover and tobacco, golden with ripening wheat, barley and oats, crimson with apples. When I visited the farm I had my choice of several ponies on which to ride through groves of hickories where in autumn I sometimes gathered bushels of nuts strewn in constellations across the grass.

These same hickories supplied the clear-grained wood for the hickory-smoked hams and sides of bacon hanging in the smokehouse, and also the nutmeats which went into Aunt Lillie's special stuffing for Thanksgiving turkeys, and her hickory-nut-gooseberry jam which made every breakfast a feast.

Pumpkins grew in such abundance that only a few became pies. Mounds ten feet high among the corn shocks were hauled from the fields by the wagonload and fed to the greedy pigs. With fifty-two cows being milked each morning and night the family was never short of milk, cream, fresh-churned butter or cottage cheese. And in the vast cellar, safely stored for the winter, were barrels of many varieties of apples, hundreds of quarts of cherries, peaches, red and black raspberries, dill pickles, sweet gherkins, bread-and-butter pickles, canned tomatoes, peas and green beans, plus bins of sand filled with beets, carrots, white turnips and ruta-bagas. Who could imagine that anyone in the world would ever again be hungry?

Gladys was city-bred, but had experienced similar pleasant occa-sions while visiting various midwestern farms when she was a child. Both of us have always looked back on those years as a re-cent golden age, when there seemed to be little or no poverty in our fertile area, and when the country was still protected by the Atlantic and Pacific oceans and by rising farm prices and limitless hope for the future.

The late 1920's and early 1930's furnished a contrast. Farm prices had slumped long before the stock market. My father was soon in financial difficulties, and I had let him "borrow" my total life savings. I earned my way through the first two years at the University of Chicago working nights, weekends and sum-mers, but also editing the campus literary magazine. Gladys and I were married at the end of my sophomore year and were so much in love that our poverty did not seem too high a price to pay for the joy of living, working and studying together. In my senior year, on a momentous day in February 1929, my first book was published simultaneously in America, England and Germany and our son David was born.

In June of that year I joined the staff of the *Chicago Daily News* as a cub reporter. Newspaper salaries in those days would be rejected by most relief clients at the present time. But thirty-five dollars a week was luxury compared to the lot of the veterans selling apples on the street corners, standing in breadlines or living in the Hoovervilles which sprang up all around the city of Chicago. It was not until I became Literary Editor of the paper (at the age of twenty-six) that I achieved a salary comparable to that of Carl Sandburg in the adjoining office—the munificent sum of one hundred dollars a week.

By this time we were saving money, and were able to pay for Arielle's arrival with a check rather than on the installment plan.

Although we took annual trips to New York, lived in a comfortable suburb, attended an irreducible minimum of literary parties and saw the new plays and art exhibits, we were (and still are) essentially country people. The most interesting individuals we met were not the celebrated authors but the characters in their books. And we remembered the serenity and security of an earlier way of life which will probably never return.

With my royalties from an early novel entitled *Plowing on Sunday,* we made a down payment on a twenty-five-acre vacation place in southern Michigan. For several hundred feet we bordered a clear little lake.

My summer hours by this time were rather flexible. For three days of the week I labored in my Chicago office and in the composing room, making up my pages. For the other four days I was in Michigan where we read the new books I was preparing to review. Gladys and I often sat with a book in one hand and a fishing rod in the other.

The lakeside farm, which had been tilled for eighty years, had many hidden assets which are seldom to be found with a newer home. Forty tall pine trees and two acres of smooth lawn surrounded the white farmhouse which we had remodeled. Rosebushes of many varieties bordered the drive and garden paths. Beds of asparagus, rhubarb and strawberries provided us with all that we could eat, give to friends or preserve. There were so many mature cherry trees loaded with both red and black varieties that even the robins and bluejays could not cope with the entire crop. A huge quince bush produced the hard green fruit for our quince honey. In our half-acre vineyard there were seven varieties of grapes. We kept the vines well pruned and fertilized. Grateful for these annual blessings provided by some previous owner, we decided to plant a small new orchard for future generations—apples, pears and apricots, all of which flourish in this region.

More than fifty hours a week were spent in reading, writing and reviewing books, and other hours in tending the garden and mowing the big lawn. But in retrospect these seem to be confident years. Somehow we found time for swimming, fishing and playing croquet with the children, studying the birds by day and the stars at night. We called our summer place "Alfalfa and Omega" and one afternoon I wrote a magazine article by this name for *Reader's Digest* (and the *Yale Review*), thus paying off the small mortgage in about five hours.

It would be unkind to would-be authors to imply, however, that it has ever been easy for anyone to make a living as a writer. In the upper levels of the profession it takes as much skill as that needed by a surgeon or a concert pianist. And with rare exceptions the pay is meager.

I have been acquainted with most of the well-known free-lancers of America in our era. Certainly no more than forty of these have been able to support themselves without holding another job, usually in education or journalism. In the 1930's I was fortunate to have the youth and energy to hold such a job while making weekly radio broadcasts and many lectures, and also writing a book a year. Since my wife was (and is) highly literate, cooperative and frugal, we managed to live comfortably and even accumulate a small stake.

In the spring of 1940 we began to yearn for a larger farm, one nearer to our suburban home and capable of sustaining a herd of Jersey cows. The children wanted a riding horse, plus ducks and chickens and lambs and all the other animals that usually demand a full-time tenant or a farm manager.

We found an attractive and fertile quarter section in northern Illinois, acquired seventy-five pure-bred Jerseys, dug a deep swimming hole in a little river which crossed one of the pastures and were able to spend almost every weekend and vacation on the property. The house and huge dairy barns had to be remodeled, water systems installed, many fences built and fields limed, fertilized and prepared for alfalfa and corn. Sometimes the monthly bills were frightening. But it was ample repayment when the sleek, fawnlike calves began to arrive and when the full-uddered cows were grazing contentedly in the lush pastures.

Our little Kentucky-bred mare, half-sister of a champion, was as swift as a swallow and as mischievous as a kitten.

When, in the year 1943, a New York newspaper offered me its Literary Editorship, which with syndicate rights would greatly multiply my salary at the *Chicago Daily News,* it seemed an offer too enticing to refuse. But to gain the willing consent of the children to such a drastic move we had to promise to bring east with us their beloved riding horse, three of their favorite Jersey heifers and a clutter of cats. One moving van would carry the furniture and several thousand books. A second truck would follow filled with livestock.

Luckily Gladys and I were in our vigorous mid-thirties and not easily daunted by obstacles. We hesitated a moment, however, when we found that four hundred laying hens came with this New Jersey estate. But even the chickens delighted the children.

When we finally saw the inside of the house with its five bedrooms and three baths, living room, music room, library and study, we capitulated completely. The real estate broker is still relating incredulously that this was the first and last time he ever sold such a property in less than one hour.

We soon added many-paned picture windows to give us better views of the little lake, the forest and Tea Mountain; and here we lived happily for several years before building a more spacious house of native stone and white clapboard, paneled with walnut from our own woods. This was on the same property, but at the foot of the lake beside our larger waterfall.

However, before those easier years arrived, we were a busy family. Both farm and domestic labor were in short supply around Morristown during World War II. We had been farm owners rather than operators in Illinois, enjoying our animals without doing any of the farm chores. Now we had maneuvered ourselves into a wild but wonderful way of life that kept everyone busy from dawn to dark.

In New York I supervised a staff of three, wrote a daily column and turned out a weekly book page plus special holiday issues which sometimes ran to a full tabloid section. Almost immediately we had twenty-four other metropolitan papers using my syndicated material, thus reaching an estimated audience of about eight million readers. Later I accepted an attractive supplementary offer to become the permanent Master of Ceremonies of *Books on Trial,* broadcast over WMGM, lining up the celebrities for the program and presiding as the black-robed judge. This meant spending every Tuesday evening in New York. In addition I continued to write books and magazine articles, and for a time helped Walt Disney create my first film, based on my best-selling novel, *So Dear to My Heart.* Meanwhile, back at the ranch:

We had miscalculated the calving date of the heifers, and were delighted but also slightly dismayed when three charming and rambunctious little bulls were born to Diana, Phoebe and Aphrodite. I had not milked a cow in more than twenty years. But a cow that needs to be milked needs to be milked. I taught my cooperative son and daughter the not too simple art of extracting milk from the not always willing cows. We then fed the livestock, cleaned the stables, fed and watered the chickens, gathered the eggs and came to the house to eat a farm-sized breakfast that Gladys had prepared.

Swiftly then the children bathed and dressed for school, I showered and dressed for the office, Gladys delivered the children to their schools and me to the 8:15 on the Lackawanna, and returned to weigh, buff and package twenty dozen eggs before starting her housework. The children returned from school and I from the office to again milk the cows and do the other evening chores.

It was good for all of us, I am sure, but I can remember days when we were too tired to fish trout in our streams or swim in the lake. In time we drastically reduced our livestock and found moments to study our ninety-six varieties of birds of passage or residence, the spring flowers and many gentle animals ranging in size from chipmunks to deer, that moved through the green shadows of our forest.

We could hear raccoons every night along the creek, but we seldom saw one. They were watching us, however, because we were raising two of their prime delicacies—chickens and sweet corn.

One night we were awakened by the terrified squawking of our hens. "Help, help! Murder! We're being slaughtered!"

In pajamas and slippers we rushed down the stairway, preparing to do battle. David grabbed a baseball bat. Gladys found flashlights. Arielle reached for the octagonal-barreled Winchester repeater which had been used for nothing but target practice since I was twelve.

*The lady of the
house also
packaged
the eggs*

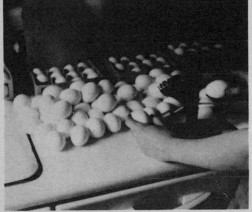

"No, Arielle," her mother said, "and particularly not at night."

"Remember, Arielle," I admonished, "we kill no living thing."

"Not even weasels, Daddy?"

"Not even weasels."

"But you *did* say snapping turtles, because they get our wild ducklings."

"This isn't a snapping turtle."

"Well, okay," Arielle protested, "but I'll bet I can equal you next time we shoot at targets."

We hurried up the hill wondering how any creature could penetrate such a building. When we switched on the light we saw a handsome raccoon, complete with bandit mask. He had killed a *single* bird—not unusual in my observation.

The corner of a broken windowpane told the story—an opening not more than four inches square. Somehow this big, furry fellow had squeezed through that aperture. But in making a wise and hasty retreat he had run into difficulties. He was dragging the chicken by one leg, and in that position the plump hen, legs aspraddle, would not go through the opening. Quick as a flash he changed the position of the bird. His glowing, intelligent eyes and sensitive hands solved the problem immediately. Dragging the hen neck first, he slipped her easily through the broken window.

"A very bright character," we all agreed.

We hold no malice toward our wild neighbors with whom we are prepared to share almost everything we raise or grow. If the field mice need a few of our tulip bulbs, or the hungry deer nip the leaves and flowers, that is their primordial privilege. When the crows pilfer some of our seed corn and the robins raid our cherries, we are philosophical. After all, they were among the first inhabitants of our valley, earlier than even the Indians. If there

is one religion for which I would tithe, it is the simple but pro-found religion of nature.

When sweet corn comes into milk, however, raccoons demand more than a tithe from the small family garden. On a nationwide basis, and considering the billions of harvested bushels of field corn, raccoon damage is infinitesimal. But let a sweet-corn patch adjoin deep woods as did ours and the havoc may be extensive.

The raccoons were watching our oncoming corn crop as closely as we were. They had pulled down an experimental stalk or two to see how the ears were forming. One afternoon David brought to the house several perfect ears and we decided that on the morrow we would pick one or two dozen and have a feast. The raccoons anticipated us, however, and during the night took nearly a fifth of the crop. From the footprints in the dust, a mother and several kits had dined royally. We left a few immature ears for the raccoons, but were wise enough to harvest immediately all the corn that was ready for eating or for freezing. No wonder raccoons like sweet corn, we said, as we buttered the hot and golden ears.

Raccoons are gourmets if they have the chance. A crayfish tastes much like its salt-water cousin, the lobster; minnows are at least as palatable as sardines, and few would deny that chicken and sweet corn are delicacies. Why then do raccoons have a passion for opening garbage pails?

David and the raccoons were watching the sweet corn

Apparently it is due to curiosity as much as necessity.

An unopened package or box is always irresistible. So is an unopened door or drawer (to the more experienced raccoon who has learned to manipulate simple knobs and latches). The raccoon's prehensile hands are endlessly busy feeling the shallows of lakes and streams for crayfish, hellgrammites, polliwogs, salamanders, minnows and small shellfish. The water evidently increases the sensitivity of his flexible digits. He has no need during his fishing for the use of his luminous, night-seeing eyes. Usually he gazes off into the moonlight as his hands progress along the bottom with an alternating, pumping motion. No crayfish hole remains unexplored, and no shining object is left uninvestigated. Round pebbles are so delightful to the raccoon that he will roll them between his hands for minutes at a time, apparently deriving the tactile pleasure that human beings experience in fingering a smooth bit of jade or a string of pearls.

Carl Burger, one of America's finest nature illustrators and an avid trout fisherman, tells of a canoe trip into the North Woods that produced an unusual raccoon incident. The canoes had been drawn up on the shore, and the duffel tossed in a pile several feet from the campfire. Usually a canvas tarpaulin was used to cover the extra food, clothing and camping equipment. But on this clear evening, the tired fishermen had neglected this precaution. After a hearty supper they had crawled into their sleeping bags around the fire and dropped asleep. Carl lay awake for a time, looking up at the stars and breathing the pine-scented air. Then he heard the trilling and churring of a pair of raccoons. Big-eyed and bushy-tailed they came softly into the firelight to examine the entrancing pile of duffel. The shining lid of a quart jar of citrus fruit attracted them immediately, but how to open it? They seemed to be holding a conference for a few moments. Then one raccoon wrapped his arms around the glass jar, while the other swiftly learned the trick of unscrewing the metal top. Soon there was no citrus fruit for the fishermen's breakfast.

Raccoons enjoy the nightly puzzle of removing the lids of garbage cans. But they also often need the contents to survive. Most towns, suburbs and cities have no corn fields and no crayfish so the raccoons find food where they can—adapting themselves to a new environment.

The raccoon's keen sense of smell will invariably tell him if fresh scraps of meat or fish are in the garbage can. It has been said that the good food thrown away by Americans would completely feed some starving nation. Several million raccoons know this to be true and have altered their habits to take advantage of our waste. But they are selective, avoiding anything that smells decayed.

Our garbage can was hidden by a hedge, but it was not hidden from the raccoons, and it was visible from two of our windows. We had yard lights that illuminated the area, and one evening, while I was watching, a mother raccoon and her four kits, perhaps the very ones that had raided our corn field, came to visit. She taught her children an important lesson—how to open a garbage can. She then tipped it over so the kits could share the feast, and they busily unwrapped every package in the can except those containing coffee grounds. Naturally I was delighted, but felt a little remiss. Was this any way to treat our guests? We should have followed the etiquette of all conscientious raccoon-feeders and prepared an appetizing meal of leftovers.

Raccoons and other night-prowling creatures soon grow accustomed to yard lights. They also seem to show no surprise when they begin to find delicacies, unnatural to their habitat, spread out each evening on a "feeding bank."

It is much easier to coax these midnight visitors to a little rise of land than to a valley or a porch enclosed by railings. They are

born strategists, and they have a greater sense of security when they can sniff the breeze from a small eminence and see in all directions. Raccoons also use their keen sense of hearing to detect any unusual noise which might spell danger, tilting their sensitive, silver-tipped ears in one direction or another to catch sounds often too faint or too high-pitched for the human ear.

We were fortunate in having

> . . . a bank whereon the wild thyme blows
> Where oxlips and the nodding violet grows . . .

It was shaded by an ancient mountain ash, and easily mounted by wide stone steps we had laboriously constructed. At the crest was an oval of green lawn bestrewn with clover. To this bank came the gentle forest neighbors we had invited. We were much more permissive toward their dietary whims than we had been toward those of our children. These new dependents of ours could have all the sweets they wanted, were never asked to eat spinach, and often were furnished with the very items they had previously stolen, scraps of fried chicken and half-eaten ears of sweet corn.

Many windows at the back of the house opened upon this sylvan cafeteria, and we were content to view for hours this evening floor show. Our first performing guests were the same plump mother and four active kits that had raided the garbage can. She was trying to wean them at this period. Some tried to nurse and were pushed away. Some ate greedily or stood on their hind feet to wrestle like bear cubs, rolling down the slope through the flowers. One little fellow leaned against his mother continuously or played gently with her tail. All was peaceful for several evenings.

The plot became more dramatic with the appearance of a very large opossum that began to arrive at dusk. He tried to dominate the entire feeding bank. The 'possum is a marsupial which has survived for fifty million years principally through overfertility and calculated imbecility. He has two or three prehistoric parlor tricks: playing dead, hanging by his tail and opening his wide toothy mouth and hissing. Oddly enough his pretended ferocity often makes him "king of the mountain."

When the mother raccoon and her kits arrived on the fifth evening, there was the 'possum eating all the food, including some items the more fastidious raccoons might have avoided. The female raccoon warned her kits, then circled the 'possum by at least five feet. But the baby raccoons were curious. Like all young things they had to learn for themselves. Moving in to touch noses with the big marsupial, they were dismayed when he opened his alligator mouth and hissed. Four little raccoons went over backward on their ringed tails and soon were hiding behind their mother, who seemed to be saying: "What did I tell you?"

Nevertheless, raccoons and 'possums continued to feed more or less happily together until one evening a red fox slunk into the glow of the yard lights, his belly almost touching the ground. We had seen a few foxes on walks through our woods, up the trail to Tea Mountain and along an abandoned logging road. These were the first live and uncaged foxes we had seen in years, and we greatly preferred them to the pink-coated fox hunters who sometimes (and without our permission) rode through our property.

But here was a proud fox, skulking in for a bite of food. He must have been desperate to have come to our feeding bank to accept charity. Just at this moment our big female cat proved who was really "king of the mountain." She had a new litter of kittens in the barn and was a tiger mother. She dashed into the light, slapping the big dog fox on the nose until he ran for the woods with his tail between his legs. She also slapped the 'possum and hissed at the raccoons. This was a rare show of violence.

Fawn hidden in foliage

Mostly we have found that animals feed together without serious conflict, a version of the Biblical "Peaceable Kingdom." But flares of temper are also to be expected and understood. They happen, however, far more frequently among the highest of primates.

During that first year in our enchanted forest we saw more wild ducks, deer, raccoons, gray and red foxes, mink, squirrels, chipmunks and other four-footed creatures than I had seen during

OPPOSITE / *Mallard hen and her reflection*

my entire boyhood in Wisconsin. On logs that had fallen across Primrose Brook we lay looking into the deep pools where trout dappled the watery sunlight, nosing upstream over clean gravel. We scaled Tea Mountain to picnic on the peak where, from a shelf of rock, we could see the towers of Manhattan.

What could we give the children more than this, and understanding affection? Obviously our only lack was a dog. I had met Eric Knight through our mutual publisher, and the whole family had enjoyed his book *Lassie Come Home*. Long before Hollywood and television vulgarized that classic, we had become fans of the original Lassie.

The nearest probable source of excellent collies was the Albert Payson Terhune line, cherished and improved near Pompton Lakes, New Jersey. Terhune had died the previous year, and his widow had ceased to breed the six or seven dogs she kept in his memory. But near their estate was a kennel dealing almost exclusively in Sunnybank collies. It was but a short drive to Pompton Lakes and the beginning of a long and memorable experience.

Since a good dog is faithful to his master for life, a good dog owner should be equally faithful. Unfortunately for such a relationship, human beings have a life-span about seven or eight times that of the average dog. We wish that we could say that the adolescent collie, pleading with us that afternoon to take her into our lives, was the only dog we had ever loved. She deserved that honor. She had lost her puppy fat and was that utterly appealing, almost tragic thing that a collie becomes when it is a gangling teen-ager (by mankind's calendar).

The American Kennel Club Stud Book showed that she was at least as well bred as our Jerseys and our chestnut mare. But we bought Lassie for no such reason. Like an admirable mutt named Curly who had saved my life five times before I reached the age of three, and like Wowser, the huge St. Bernard who had protected all my boyhood pets, Lodestone Bryn Gola Lassie, "Sable with white markings," would have remained an aristocrat even had she lacked papers.

There was never any doubt which of the young collies we would choose, since she had already chosen us. As Arielle and David consoled her, she stood with her front paws on the woven wire, talking, asking, singing the collie language understood by all sensitive children. We scarcely looked at the papers or questioned the substantial price, and in a few moments she was ours.

Lassie had the sleek profile of all Sunnybank dogs, liquid eyes, delicate legs with neat white stockings and a lustrous pelt. When the wire door was opened, she bounded into our arms, licking the faces of the delighted children and yelping cries of greeting; then she bowed politely like a little lady before running in joyous circles around and around us.

She was not afraid of us. In fact she showed in every possible way that she loved us. But she had never before taken a ride in a car. On the trip homeward she lay on the back seat, paralyzed with fear. Despite all the petting and tender assurances the children could give her, she became more and more rigid and glassy-eyed. Her heart was beating, but far too faintly. We broke the speed laws getting her home.

We lifted her frail body from the car, rigid as a board. Both children were fighting back their tears. Inside the house we soaked towels in hot water to wrap around here chilling body and forced warm milk between her clenched teeth. Gladys and I gave each other a meaningful glance—we were sure we had lost her. But slowly her body became less rigid and she seemed to be able to hear our voices. She began to relax, and light and intelligence returned to her big brown eyes. She apparently realized that four affectionate people were attending her. In a few more minutes her tail wagged feebly. Then she tried a small, joyous yelp and we knew she would live.

What a charming, eccentric, devoted friend she was, the last and the best of all our dogs. She would never again ride in a car. But to leave her behind when we took a vacation was to risk losing her. Our neighbors tried to feed her but she would fast in grieving remembrance of us. When we returned she would crawl pitifully to our feet, turn on her back and cry for half an hour at a time.

Those who say that all intelligence has been bred out of modern collies never met our Lassie. She knew each of us by name, and had an understanding vocabulary of at least thirty words. Perhaps she could not have duplicated the sheep-herding proclivities of the great "border collies" of southern Scotland and northern England, but no dog could have been more devoted to her own small family—meaning Gladys, the children and myself. When we went swimming in the lake she was certain we would perish and went racing back and forth across the crest of the waterfall crying out to us, in very plain language, "You'll drown, you'll certainly drown; but I'll come to your rescue."

She never hunted a living animal, and never injured a human being. She would follow a meadow mouse with her long, aristocratic nose, highly interested but not as a hunter—for she never harmed a mouse, a chipmunk nor the many kittens she helped to rear. Baby ducks crawled into her golden fur for warmth or poised on her head. But despite her tenderness, she thought that she must protect us. So she bravely barked at all raccoons and deer. Thus, for about ten years we were deprived of the very friends

OPPOSITE / *Young things—Arielle, Lassie and puppy*

we had hoped to make in this valley. The wilderness creatures (not knowing that Lassie was utterly harmless) stayed some distance from the house.

The years rolled on, rich with experience and emotion. Books came from my typewriter, the children finished high school with salutatorian averages. Arielle went on to Swarthmore and David to Princeton, where they graduated with honors. We grew older, and so, alas, did our faithful collie.

We planted many flowering trees, built our new house on several levels beside the waterfall, attended the graduation exercises at Princeton and Swarthmore and began to think of early retirement. But we always believed, even with the children launched on successful careers, that we would have one final dependent, Lassie.

She did not mean to fail us, I am sure. It was not her fault that she began to try to climb the back steps five feet south of where they were. Finally we knew with terrible assurance what we had only guessed before. She was completely blind. Our very wise and tender veterinarian told us that she also had incurable cancer, and advised us to steel ourselves for the last kindness we could perform.

There was a hurricane raking the valley on that day. But we paid no heed to the crashing trees as we held Lassie in our arms and the doctor inserted the merciful needle. She was licking our hands as she again became rigid and glassy-eyed. We have never had the courage to own another dog.

Nature, however, tries to heal many wounds. The deer and the raccoons now began to come to our very door. And twin raccoon kits, named Flora and Fauna, helped to ease our loss during the year following Lassie's death.

TWO

Flora's First Year

There are several reasons why raccoons love our valley. There are, of course, the springs and streams and the little lake. There are beechnuts and acorns. And there are wild pastures where crickets and grasshoppers abound. Furthermore there is the comforting sense of relative security which all wild animals feel in an area protected from hunters.

For the den-seeking raccoon there is yet another irresistible attraction. Ours is a climax forest of oaks, beeches, walnuts, maples and other deciduous varieties with only a sprinkling of pines and hemlocks. Raccoons greatly prefer these woods to even a virgin stand of evergreen timber. Trees such as ours mean not only food but shelter. The softer maples, red oaks, sycamores and elms are more susceptible to injury and decay than most of the conifers.

This tragedy to the tree is a blessing to the raccoon, which despite all his other virtues has never learned to build a nest for himself without some aid, usually from inclement weather and other forest dwellers. It is true that, lacking den trees, raccoons will raise their kits in small caves, woodchuck holes, old boathouses, suburban attics or even an abandoned osprey nest. But if an impartial pollster were to ask all the mother raccoons in America one simple question, they would receive an almost unanimous answer: "Give me a good den tree!"

The location of the door to a den varies in altitude from ground level to sixty or seventy feet above the forest floor. The entrance is usually four inches or more in diameter, and the inner cavity two or three cubic feet or larger. Sometimes decay within the major branches gives the raccoon safe galleries leading to other rooms. Most raccoons, however, avoid "chimney trees," which have a hole at the base, running up the trunk and out at the top. Possibly they dislike the rain and snow that drift in from above, a cause of pneumonia in raccoons. It would probably be giving them too much credit to suggest that they intelligently avoid such hollow trees because they sometimes become incinerators for whole litters of raccoons, frequently including the devoted mother. A ground fire running through the forest seldom injures large, sound trees, but it does send flames roaring up the chimney trees.

A good raccoon den is usually many years in the making. It may start with a lightning bolt injuring the tree, or with a limb being torn from the trunk during a storm. Unless the tree can quickly heal its wound, rain and snow seep in, and alternate freezing and thawing damage an inner portion of the trunk itself. Bacteria and insects begin to feed upon the wood. So do colonies of woodeating ants, which soon attract the bright and noisy flickers.

The particular den of which I am speaking was twenty feet above the ground. Nuthatches in search of grubs had begun to deepen the hole shortly after we arrived in the valley. In 1945, when the opening was still small, a pair of bluebirds used the hollow in which to lay their pale blue eggs and rear their young. Later inhabitants included downy woodpeckers, their larger cousins, the hairy woodpeckers, and finally a handsome pair of eighteen-inch flame-crested woodchoppers, the pileated—largest of all woodpeckers except the ivory-billed (now probably extinct). Eventually squirrels stored acorns in the enlarging cavity. Finally a female raccoon whom we had named Moonlight chose this den. We knew she was there not only because we had seen her enter and leave, but because, one autumn afternoon, when we knocked on the base of the tree with a large stick, Moonlight looked out to see who was disturbing the peace.

Raccoons are avid eaters during the spring and early summer, but they become almost insatiable during the autumn. Moonlight had been feasting on wild grapes, moving with ease through the vine-draped trees to reach the frosty purple clusters. We had seen her raking delicate fingers through the drifted leaves, where she captured and devoured many crimson salamanders. When acorns began to shower down like hail, Moonlight consumed them in surprising quantities. She was bold enough to come to the back porch of our new house, where we now fed not only raccoons but well-behaved skunks, 'possums and an occasional fox.

One autumn evening when a cold rain was falling, Moonlight chased all the cats out of their weatherproof and insulated house, at the far end of the porch, and lolled in luxury on the folded quilt while looking from the circular doorway, obviously enjoying the discomfort of the evicted pets. We knew that she had a snug den of her own and saw no reason why she should oust the cats. But Moonlight was a personality. She loved her creature comforts, was absolutely dauntless and remarkably willful. When the rain ceased, this big female raccoon squeezed out of the cat house and cheerfully trundled up the hill to her den. Her evening had been a success.

Raccoons put on many pounds in October and November, as though they instinctively understand that cold and miserable weather will soon confine them to their hollow trees. They dislike wind and snow, and will usually avoid either if possible. After the temperature has dropped a few degrees below freezing they much prefer to curl in a furry ball and go to sleep, living for weeks on their stored fat. While it is true that raccoons do not hibernate in the scientific sense, and that their temperature does not plummet as does that of the woodchuck, they do drowse away most of the winter.

All through the cold months we looked for her tracks in the snow at the foot of her tree but found them only once during a January thaw. Apparently she had dug a few acorns from beneath the leaves and then had returned to her den.

In late February, however, not only *her* tracks but the larger ones of male raccoons were to be seen in the slush and mud. Moonlight was having visitors.

It is believed that raccoons have a double standard. Male raccoons are quite obviously polygamous and will travel for miles seeking mates. Female raccoons are more fastidious and will drive away suitors until the right one happens along. Sometimes a female is so unreasonable in her demands that she may find no mate during the entire season.

Moonlight, who had a mind of her own, must have slapped or nipped a number of importuning males, for the raccoon tracks at the foot of her tree were numerous. In early March, however, she evidently denned up for a couple of weeks with a raccoon who had caught her fancy. Sixty-three days after the mating, her kits were born. Meanwhile, all over America, in every continental state of the Union, and from southern Alaska and Canada to central America, other females were making their choice of males, then awaiting the happy inevitable. And although raccoons in Dixie mate a little earlier in the season, the period of gestation is always the same.

Spring days now engulfed the valley—wild geese V-ing northward over our woods and little lake, mallards and wood ducks visiting our protected water. The red-winged blackbirds with their liquid notes came to swing and sway on our willows, and male song sparrows arrived, each staking out a nesting territory. In another few weeks, flowers of a dozen varieties bloomed everywhere. Anemones and violets by the millions rimmed the pathways through our forest. The peepers began to sing. And new life stirred within many mother animals.

As Moonlight grew heavier she confined her foraging trips to an area within a few hundred feet of her den. She searched the margin of the lake to catch minnows and crayfish, and visited our feeding pan on the back porch. She also ate quantities of last autumn's acorns. But she was not as combative as she had been six months earlier. She did less growling and hissing at our cats and seemed to be having inward thoughts. Then during the first week in May we did not see her for a few days, but we believed that all was well. We were almost certain she had given birth to her litter of blind, soft-furred, purring infants.

Raccoon litters vary in number from two to seven. In our valley three or four babies are usual, but twins are not uncommon. The mothers have six teats and can provide rich milk at each of these life-giving fountains. But we have noticed that the smaller the family the plumper the kits.

At birth the raccoons weigh a scant two ounces. But they are lusty feeders and grow quite rapidly. They have little to do ex-

cept sleep and eat and curl up together for warmth. They open their eyes in about three weeks to get their first dim view of each other and of their comfortable home.

It is surprising how early they experience their first competition. Like tiny kittens they will claw and struggle for a favorite nipple. When barely able to see, they begin to practice clumsy wrestling holds—growling almost inaudibly. A moment later they will be cuddled together purring peacefully.

A good den tree furnishes almost complete safety. There may be enemies in the great outside world (which they soon begin to view from the doorway of the den). But here in the dusky hollow of soft and rotted wood, guarded by their fiercely defensive mother, they need fear no evil. Even when their protectress leads them forth on their first expedition into the forest there are few predators to attack them. Here in New Jersey, where the last cougar was shot more than a hundred years ago, little raccoons have only two forest enemies, the relatively rare great horned owl and the even rarer bobcat.

When the very capable female raccoon (who raises her young with no help from the male) calls to her ten-week-old children, their only real apprehension is that they might fall as they cautiously back down the tree to the ground.

We were fortunate in seeing what may have been the first adventure into the unknown by Moonlight's handsome kits. They were two in number, one slightly larger and more lightly colored than the other, and almost immediately they gave us a clue as to their personalities.

There was an air of assurance in the larger raccoon that was

OPPOSITE / Upper left: *rue anemone*   Upper right: *white trillium*
Lower left: *yellow lady slipper*   Lower right: *marsh marigold*

Bobcat   *Horned owl*

lacking in the somewhat smaller sibling. The bolder baby followed her mother quite readily. The more timid one clung to the trunk of the tree and began to cry in terror. Moonlight churred encouragement. This cheered the bigger youngster, who in a final scramble reached the ground. But the stranded offspring only wailed the louder. Plainly annoyed, but still the protective mother, Moonlight practically galloped up the tree, took her whimpering child by the nape of the neck, as a cat will take a kitten, and carried it down to safety.

We were permitted to watch this spectacle late one afternoon. Raccoons are normally nocturnal animals—but not in all instances. Darkness is a cloak of protection to these night prowlers whose five acute senses are so perfectly attuned to the world of the bat, the nighthawk and the owl. But another survival instinct of the raccoon is his great adaptability. If conditions alter, he alters his habits accordingly. My pet raccoon, Rascal, who slept and played with me when I was a boy, obviously enjoyed my companionship. So he changed his schedule to suit mine, sleeping most of the night in my bed and remaining awake and active most of the day. Correspondents on both the Atlantic and Pacific coasts confirm my own observation that seaboard raccoons alter their hours to conform to the constantly shifting tides. At ebb tide, a multitude of marine life remains stranded on tidal flats and ocean beaches. This is a windfall to the bright and always hungry raccoons who

Flora's first big adventure

like to scrounge their shore dinners the easy way. No matter what time of the day or night the tide goes out, the raccoons move in. They are taking no chance of letting other banqueters arrive first. Many people who feed wild raccoons have slowly moved the evening meal forward until they are able to lure their guests into keeping an afternoon appointment.

One other element enters the picture. If raccoons feel as protected as they do in our valley, they are more likely to venture forth in the late afternoon to start their evening feeding early.

Since Moonlight had little to fear from us, we were able to stand within about fifty feet of the base of her den tree while she began to teach her children their first important lesson in earning their own living.

A recent rain which had softened the ground had brought earthworms near the surface. As Moonlight led her kits down a mossy, fern-fringed ravine, she paused in a likely spot and began to dig in the leafmold. This was a new game to her babies, who soon were digging diligently. When Moonlight uncovered a big nightcrawler, her larger and lustier infant pounced upon it and began to eat. Moonlight wanted to devour the worm herself. But something told her that unless she let her children have a portion of the food, she would never be able to wean them. Meanwhile the smaller kit, who had been rolling a smooth pebble between its hands, realized it was missing something. When it tried to nibble the other end of the worm, however, fierce little growls from the larger child forced a retreat. Frustrated in this contest, the lesser infant began nursing, but Moonlight, for the first time perhaps, pushed it away. Looking and feeling quite rejected, the little raccoon lay down on a cushion of green moss and began to suck a paw.

Well, that's the way to find earthworms, Moonlight seemed to be saying. Now for another lesson.

We followed as closely as we thought wise, remaining partly hidden by clumps of rhododendrons and stepping lightly on the carpet of leaves.

The next stop for the raccoon family was a big rotting log that lay beside the rivulet of spring water. Moonlight spoke to her children and began scratching strips of loose bark from the decaying wood. Another fine game, thought the young raccoons, and they too pulled bark with their claws and their sharp teeth. Under the bark were a multitude of grubs and insects. Since Mother enjoyed them, they must be good to eat. Odd-tasting but delightful, thought the little raccoons, guzzling grubs and licking up insects.

Come along my children, Moonlight churred, and led them on down the ravine to sample one of the most succulent foods they would find all afternoon. Our woods abound in berries—wild strawberries, blueberries, raspberries, blackberries and, most tantalizing of all, wineberries. The wineberry, which makes excellent jelly, looks and tastes something like a tame red raspberry except that it has far more tang to its sweetness. It has another advantage for berry-pickers—human or raccoon. The "thorns" on the vines are so soft that they never prick. This was the height of the wineberry season, with the pliable canes bending low with their burden of fruit. All three raccoons were soon gorging.

Save some room for minnows and crayfish, Moonlight seemed to be saying as she led her reluctant children away from the berries and out upon a little sandbar where the rivulet entered the shallow upper end of our small lake.

And now began one of the most important lessons any raccoon mother can teach her offspring in those few short months she has to bring them from infancy to maturity. It is the exciting art of fishing.

She had purposely brought them to the shallows because here

were to be found frogs, mussels, minnows and crayfish. All raccoons, even little ones, can swim. But apparently they cannot dive. What they really prefer to do is wade and dabble while gazing at the treetops.

Up to this point the raccoon kits had been willing pupils. But now they hung back for a few minutes, perplexed and fearful. Mother seemed safe and happy, wading over the sand and gravel and occasionally grasping, washing and eating a minnow. But the little ones were not certain. It looked deep and dangerous to them.

Then the personality equation appeared again, so sharply we laughed aloud. The smaller baby began running up and down the shore crying piteously to its mother—pleading with her to come back to solid land. The big bold child waded in and began to explore with its little front paws. In a memorable moment, it grabbed, nearly lost, then grabbed again a plump polliwog. There were hundreds of polliwogs in the lake, a few of which would survive to become bullfrogs. But there was an excess which became legitimate food for fish, herons and raccoons.

True, there would be one less bass fiddle thrumming across the water on some subsequent summer evening. But at this moment we could only revel in the excitement and sense of triumph of a brave, three-pound raccoon who had caught its first polliwog.

They were so much the spirit of our forest, so much the essence of it, that they deserved woodland names.

"Flora and Fauna," Gladys suggested.

So Big Flora and Little Fauna became important new characters in our daily lives.

A few afternoons later Moonlight and her two children made a formal call. The extrovert mother came directly to the back door and peered through the screen. Flora and Fauna seemed far less

assured. They climbed an old fence post, and from this safe observation point weighed the dangers of this new adventure.

We had not yet prepared the evening meal which we invariably leave for raccoons and other wayfarers, so Moonlight decided to help herself to the sunflower seeds in the bird feeder. This hangs from a slender limb of a redbud tree which arches over the porch, and in every season of the year attracts chickadees, titmice, nuthatches, downy woodpeckers and a host of other birds, but also marauding squirrels and an occasional raccoon.

Flora and Fauna watched fascinated as Moonlight ventured out on the branch, which began to bend under her weight. It has always amazed us that raccoons, weighing up to twenty pounds and more, can perform such high-wire acrobatics. Not as nimble as a squirrel, and often as ludicrous as a circus clown, they slip, catch themselves, progress upside down along the under side of a limb, scramble up again, and, with self-assurance, amble forward to their destination.

To our knowledge, Moonlight had never previously raided the bird feeder, and was now doing so mostly to satisfy her curiosity. She could see the sunflower seeds through the glass panels, and perhaps she could smell them. In less than a minute she had learned how to lift the hinged roof. Clinging to the limb with her hind feet, she began taking seeds with her nimble hands. These she chewed and savored with great satisfaction as she dug deeper and deeper into the supply. Then she paused and examined minutely the manner in which the feeder was attached to the bough. We had fastened a hook of stiff wire to the limb, and the bird feeder hung by a metal ring suspended from the hook. This was a kindergarten problem for our wise old raccoon who

OPPOSITE / *Flora and Fauna make a formal call*

promptly lifted the ring from the hook and dropped the bird feeder. Luckily the glass did not smash, but the roof swung open strewing a pound of seeds on the top step of the porch.

The little raccoons could not resist such a powerful inducement. They swarmed down the fence post and up the steps to join the feast. Above them in the redbud tree a bluejay scolded loudly, and soon a pair of chickadees, who often eat from our hands, came darting in, snatching a plump seed on each aerial raid.

During the next four weeks we were continually entertained by this family of raccoons. We saw them attempting to rob a crow's nest, and witnessed a complete defeat as the mother crow, joined by a posse of a dozen others, drove the bandits down the tree. We observed them unearthing snapping turtle eggs from a sandbar in the lake and watched them dine to repletion on these delicacies, a favorite food of skunks as well as raccoons. Fauna, although still the more timorous one, had at last overcome fear of the water and had learned to fish. It was high time! Raccoons at the age of fourteen weeks are rapidly acquiring their forty adult teeth including their four large, needle-sharp incisors. The discomfort these teeth give to the female raccoon doubtless hastens the weaning process. The youngsters from this point on have no choice but to fish, forage and fend for themselves.

Apparently in the animal kingdom, the greater the intelligence, the wider the variability in the personality of the individuals. Moonlight had a high IQ even for so bright a species as the raccoon, but she had a temper to match, and we had decided against letting her come into the house and also against feeding her from our hands. Now watching her on the back porch each afternoon and evening with her two growing kits, we were aware that she had given Flora much of her spirit, dash and determination, while Fauna was another sort entirely, an affectionate, shy little moonling who was always leaning against his mother, or playing gently with a moth or a blossom.

By this age it is easy to tell the sex of a raccoon if it is obliging enough to sit up and be viewed. As we had surmised, Flora, the larger, bolder youngster, was a girl raccoon, and timid Fauna was a boy. We had noticed similar differences so often that we had come to consider it a basic sex pattern, due perhaps to the fact that the females mature much more rapidly than the males. A very high percentage of all females bear their first litters of young at the age of twelve months. Only a small percentage of the males are ready to take a mate the first year, although my boyhood pet Rascal had done so. By the second year, however, the males have overtaken the females in size and fertility, and frequently outweigh them by several pounds.

Flora and Fauna were running true to form in this respect and demonstrated their differences on almost every visit. Flora had acquired a mischievous habit of climbing into the big feeding pan and covering as much of the evening meal as possible while she ate. She would growl at Fauna and even at her mother when either came near. Fauna ran in circles around the pan making little cries of frustration and distress. Finally he discovered the only riposte to his sister's raccoon-in-the-manger technique. He would crawl under Flora, snatch a chunk of meat and dash away to eat in peace.

Moonlight would tolerate only so much of Flora's nonsense, then she would growl at her daughter and, through superior strength, push her bodily out of the pan.

We began to place several dishes of food on the porch, well separated from each other so that all the raccoons could eat harmoniously. There was now less hissing and growling and more churring and purring among our free-loaders.

All went well until Empress Eugenie brought her three charming kittens to the back porch on an evening when the raccoons were already in possession. Eugenie was the most beautiful skunk that has ever honored us with a visit. She was almost entirely a sleek and glossy black except for a perfect coronet or delicate crown of white on her head, plus two pencil stripes of white on either side of her back and a white fringe at the end of her black tail. With her came her black and white kits following Indian file.

The young raccoons were now expert climbers and had no difficulty mounting the steps. The somewhat smaller baby skunks found each step an imposing barrier. But urging them on was their mother on the porch above them. Obedient, loyal and determined, they struggled up this obstacle course and were soon beside her. As each black nose, with its thin median stripe of white, made its appearance over the rim of the top step, we watched with delight from within the screen door.

Skunks, like raccoons, have almost no natural enemies in New Jersey except the horned owl, which will swoop silently upon a skunk of any size venturing through the dusky forest. Undaunted by the spray of blinding, nauseating liquid which skunks can squirt from the two scent glands under the base of the tail, the owl strikes with talons and beak, carrying the unfortunate animal to a favorite perching place where it is devoured—fur, flesh, bones, entrails, scent and all. Some of the less digestible parts are regurgitated as owl pellets, but the rest is easily assimilated.

Skunks and raccoons have so many characteristics in common that one might expect far more frequent confrontations than actually occur. The skunk's geographical distribution in North America is almost exactly the same as that of the raccoon. They live in all our continental states, and from southern Canada to Central America. Both are classed as carnivores, but in truth are omnivorous, each eating almost the same fruits, berries, insects, birds' eggs, turtle eggs and table scraps relished by the other species.

Both give birth in the spring, the skunk having a slightly briefer gestation period. Mother skunks, like mother raccoons, have six teats, and carefully nurse, protect and train their young. It is of utmost importance to the kittens of both species that they follow their mother through woodlands and meadows watching what she eats and how she hunts. They learn, among many other things, that it is better to bluff than to fight. In fact it is with great reluctance that a skunk uses its ultimate defensive weapon.

I raised several young skunks in my boyhood, and none were descented by the relatively simple operation which removes the musk glands. All of these little creatures were affectionate pets. Only once or twice did I have to burn or bury my clothes after accidents which were seldom the fault of the skunk. Usually it was the aggressive approach of a malicious boy or a stupid dog that made the little skunk start stamping and pattering its front feet—a warning that should always be taken seriously.

There are many superstitions about skunks that have no basis in fact. Picking up a skunk by the tail does not assure you of immunity. Standing in front of a skunk instead of behind it is equally futile. If a skunk arches its back, lifts its tail and begins playing a soft tattoo with its front paws you may be sure that it is wise to retreat.

We had never experienced a malodorous misfortune on our back porch, but we were well aware that both Moonlight and Eugenie were dominant females and protective mothers, not likely to confess defeat without a little bluffing. Lucky for us that we had increased the number of feeding pans! Eugenie's front paws pattered a few times, and Moonlight growled once or twice. But no showdown occurred on this occasion. The skunk mother and her brood chose the pan farthest from where the raccoons were eating, and the four skunks and three raccoons continued to feast in contentment.

I accidentally disrupted the "balanced ecology" of our valley and also the feeding pattern of Moonlight and her twins during the interesting summer of which I am writing. Leaves and sand are slowly washed into our little lake by the two trout streams that enter at the northwest corner of the pond. Once every decade or so it becomes necessary to drain the lake through an ancient flume, and dredge out some ten thousand cubic yards of silt, sand and leaves. This lowers the lake floor by nearly twelve feet, and temporarily destroys the shallow crayfishing grounds of our friends in nearby den trees.

But trust the raccoon, who is always an opportunist, to take advantage of any turn of fortune. As the shoreline receded, exposing mud flats and sandbars, not only Moonlight and her kits but several other raccoon families descended on the new bonanza. Their prints covered the lake bottom like filigree lace, mingling with other motifs—the webfooted tracks of muskrats and wild ducks, the signatures of birds as small as the spotted sandpiper and as large as the great blue heron. Snapping turtles weighing up to thirty pounds, dragging their armor across the mud, left a record of their passage resembling that left by the treads of army tanks. Much of the living history of creation from the amoeba to man was here exposed, for we too waded and explored, enjoying the sand between our toes, and leaving the plantigrade footprints of Homo sapiens.

Many of the fish escaped upstream or downstream, but enough minnows and trout were stranded in shallow pools to give the raccoons a moonlit revel. Claws of crayfish, the only part the raccoon refuses to eat, littered both sides of the stream flowing across the bottom of the pond.

For five days the big draglines and bulldozers removed about two thousand yards of sediment a day, cleaning the pond down to a hardpan of firm clay and bedrock. But at night the basin of the little lake belonged to the raccoons who devoured fish, frogs, salamanders, small turtles and even fresh-water mussels, which they open by chewing at the hinges of the shells with their sharp incisors. Flora and Fauna were enjoying a postgraduate course in the art of harvesting every variety of fresh-water food. And since the month was now September, they gorged in anticipation of their long winter siesta. Often a large raccoon at this time of the year will eat three or four pounds a day—up to one quarter of the weight of his plump body.

When the excavation was completed, we closed the flume and within twenty-four hours were able to fill the greatly deepened lake with clear, cold water pouring in from the two trout streams. Now the raccoons returned to their marginal fishing.

Our first frost that year was a mild one, nipping only the most tender of our flowers, but hastening the chemical processes that turn the maple leaves to crimson, the hickories to buckskin yellow and the oaks to shades of bronze and morocco. These colors had been present in the leaves all summer, masked by the green of the chlorophyll. But now the verdant, life-sustaining cells were dying and fading, allowing the true brilliance to blossom forth against the blue of the autumn sky.

The squirrels, wood ducks, pheasants, deer and raccoons ate bushels of acorns. Striped chipmunks, cramming their pouches with smaller seeds, worked frantically to fill their underground granaries for the winter. The goldenrod and wild asters swept across the wild pastures and along every pathway through the woods. It is always sad to say good-by to summer, but the brisk air, the burst of color and the clangor of wild geese wedging southward set our blood atingle as we roamed our valley, watching and listening.

There is, however, one aspect of this season which sends a very different chill along the spine. Hunters, responding to a primitive urge which once had meaning, begin to clean and polish their guns and purchase licenses and ammunition for the yearly slaughter of small game, waterfowl and deer. Although our acres are known as a game sanctuary, and although they adjoin the protected national park, it is a rare year in which the police do not catch at least one deer-jacker or other poacher.

Men with guns have been largely eliminated from our woods. But hunting dogs cannot read No Trespassing signs. They sometimes come alone or in packs to trail our foxes, hunt our raccoons and pull down our deer.

Late one October afternoon we heard what could only be raccoon dogs on a hot trail. My wife and I were sitting with a visitor on the terrace beside the waterfall when a frenzied commotion which raccoon hunters call "music" came faintly to our ears. We immediately took the wide path into the woods, fearing particularly for Moonlight and her three-quarters-grown kits who alone of our raccoons ventured forth by daylight.

Although we ourselves are now devoid of the hunting urge, we come of frontier stock that once killed game from necessity. Before my twelfth birthday I trapped and hunted like the rest, reliving the history of the race. This was before I matured sufficiently to understand the cruelty of mangling the paws of inoffensive animals in steel-jawed traps or blasting away with a twelve-gauge at trusting wild ducks and geese, coming in over decoys.

There were valid reasons for hunting during most of our evolution. Man was not the strongest nor was he the swiftest of the species with which he was in competition. He was no match for the cave bear, the saber-toothed tiger nor the mastodon. Had he not fashioned crude spears and other weapons he could not have defended nor fed his family.

Hunting became much less important than herding and agriculture toward the end of this long era. But until very recently (and even to this day in some remote outposts) it was needful to take wild animals for food and clothing. This furnishes no excuse to the modern "hunter," particularly the "sportsman" who shoots the vanishing polar bear from an airplane, or the trophy-seekers of Africa who, like the late Ernest Hemingway, make killing a cult.

The American frontiersman, like the American Indian, had little choice. But the lust to kill became an increasingly dangerous vice as well-fed Easterners, led by scouts like Kit Carson, all but eliminated the tens of millions of buffalo on the western plains, and as market hunters slaughtered and eventually destroyed the last of the hundreds of millions of passenger pigeons which in my grandfather's day darkened the sky for hours during their migrations.

Raccoons were in somewhat less danger of extinction. They were admired as well as hunted by the Indians who gave the species its name, meaning "he who scratches." Several great tribes venerated and paid tribute to these "little men," whom they sometimes adopted as their symbolic brothers. Like our frontiersmen the Indians relished the flesh, utilized the fat to soften leather and, long before Boone or Crockett, used the fur and ringed tail for raccoon-skin hats.

As we walked along forest paths which had once been used by the Indians, by continental troops during the Revolution and by nature-lovers down to the most recent Audubon Society bird-count, we could hear the baying of the hounds still in warm pursuit.

Moonlight was a wise old raccoon. Undoubtedly she had been trailed by dogs during previous seasons. The very fact that she had survived proved that she knew most of the subtle tricks of the trade, which she now was teaching to her children. She and the twins were probably crossing and recrossing the brook and sometimes wading upstream to break the trail. The frequent yelps of frustration from the hounds seemed to indicate that she and the kits occasionally backtracked to multiply the confusion, or climbed a tree and crossed over to another tree, to come down many feet from where the wildly excited 'coon dogs thought they had treed their quarry. Then the baying of the hounds became much fainter, and we realized that Moonlight had led the pursuers over the ridge and was circling back toward the historic site of Stark's Brigade on the far slope of Tea Mountain.

What little I know about raccoon hunting with dogs came to me from Old Bruce, an interesting character who lived in southern Indiana. Bruce was a living museum of folk ballads, many of which had been imported across the Atlantic by his Scotch-Irish ancestors. While I was at the University of Chicago I wrote a fairly extensive paper on the ballads of the southern Highlands and the manner in which they resembled (or differed from) the originals, often dating back to the reign of Queen Elizabeth I.

While my collecting never equaled that of the Lomaxes, and my singing and banjo playing offered no competition to Burl Ives, I continued my amateur interest for many years, and would go miles out of my way to meet an artist like our old friend in the Indiana hills. Bruce had two passions: playing his five-string banjo while "rared back" in his splint-bottom "settin' chair," or listening to the music of his 'coon hounds—a fine pack of Redbones, Blueticks and Black-and-Tans.

It is said that our original stringed instruments were evolved from the hunter's bow. Perhaps our horns and woodwinds came from a somewhat similar source. Stag horns and ram horns can be heard much farther than the human voice. From antiquity they have been used to call the half-wild but willing dogs which for thousands of years have joined mankind in the hunt. So it is not surprising that many of our vestigial social types play the fiddle, blow the hunting horn and insist that the baying of their dogs is "music."

Old Bruce and his cronies had once been so rugged and avid in the chase that they had plunged through the brush, brambles and cat briers, up one limestone ridge and down the next, in pursuit of their hounds. When the 'coon was treed they used lanterns or flashlights to locate the gleaming eyes. Then they either shot the unfortunate animal or shook it from the tree to let it fight valiantly to its death. Bruce had become less vigorous and more mellow with the years. He seldom actually killed a raccoon in the days when we knew him.

He would blow his bugle, which hung with his several guns on the sweetgum paneling above the fireplace. The dogs for miles around would come cross-country at the sound of the horn, and would gather in a wildly excited pack awaiting the hunt. The aging owners of these dogs followed the gravel roads and were slower in arriving.

Bruce would ask his friends if this would be a "chasin' hunt or a listnin' hunt." Since their average age was now seventy, they would usually settle for listening. Carrying their corncob pipes to the top of nearby limestone knob, they would build a fire if the evening was cool. Around this comfortable blaze they would smoke quietly half the night, identifying boastfully the crying of some beloved hound ahead of the pack, telling stories of the long ago. It was more like rural fox-hunting in parts of Missouri, with no horses or pink-coated riders, just the harmony of the hounds and the company of fellow music-lovers. Foxes must first "go to ground" before fox hounds are called in by the horn, and raccoon hounds must first bark that the 'coon is "treed." Then the hunting

Raccoons grow plump in the autumn, also wary of dogs and hunters

horn is victoriously sounded to bring in the dogs, with little major damage to dogs or quarry.

It would be comforting but inaccurate to report that all raccoon hunts are as innocent as those conducted by Bruce in his later years. On the contrary, all but a few are still a bloody business. For every hunter who carries flashbulbs and camera merely to obtain photographic evidence that his dogs have treed a raccoon, several thousand carry guns. It is estimated that approximately

one million raccoons are shot or trapped every year, largely for "sport." Only 'coon hunters are so rash as to insist that the meat is delicious. The pelts, which brought as much as eighteen dollars in the flapper and 'coonskin-coat era of the 1920's, are now hardly worth taking from the carcass, bringing about one dollar a hide. Since a good raccoon dog costs at least one hundred and twenty-five dollars and will seldom account for more than three or four raccoons a season, the economics of this sort of hunting may well cause part of the poverty in Appalachia and the Ozarks where "they sometimes feed their dogs better than their children." Old Bruce used to admit, " 'Coon hunting is a sort of midnight madness."

While dogs, plus human hunters, make a deadly combination, dogs hunting alone are far less dangerous to the quarry. There is nothing they can do about a treed raccoon if there is no man there to shoot it. Furthermore the raccoon, normally a peaceful animal, puts up a tremendous fight if cornered. Pound-for-pound he can lick any dog that ever lived.

There is another great advantage that the experienced raccoon has over a dog if he can lure it into deep water. The dog in its frenzy may dive in after the raccoon, often to its destruction. A big raccoon can climb on the head of his pursuer and hold him under until he drowns. Apparently that was the strategy Moonlight was now planning. She seemed to be headed our way, and the frantic baying of the hounds showed that they were very close behind her on the trail.

We began hurrying toward the sound of the hunt, and just as we rounded a curve on the path that skirts the lake, we saw Moonlight, furiously at bay while the hounds moved in warily for the kill. She had obviously left the kits behind and was performing the classic maneuver of most raccoon mothers—leading danger away from her young.

We shouted at the dogs and began pelting them with stones, which distracted them just long enough for Moonlight to plunge into the lake and start swimming for the other shore. The dogs would probably have followed except for our shouting, but they were not giving up the hunt so easily. I was not their master, and they had no intention of minding me while a raccoon was in sight. Instead they raced around the edge of the lake hoping to catch Moonlight on the far shore. But she was there long before them and galloping up a far ridge of hills with the dogs again in pursuit.

We listened for nearly half an hour until we could no longer hear the baying and yelping. We could merely hope that Moonlight was safe. But we never saw her again, nor did we see Fauna.

Sometimes raccoon families regroup after a hunt, if any are alive to do so. Our little family did not, and we could only be sure that one of the three was alive. A few nights later Flora came to the back porch for food, but instead of the confident raccoon she had been, she snatched a chunk of meat and ran back into the woods.

Evidently nothing seemed safe to her that disturbing autumn. After the next rain we looked for her tracks at the foot of the old den tree, but no raccoon was living in that tree so recently occupied. Apparently she had tried many dens, seeking one in which she could feel secure.

At last one afternoon we saw her emerging from an entirely different den in a much larger tree, and decided that she had chosen to spend the cold months in its friendly hollow. She would not be as warm as she would have been if her mother and brother had curled up with her in the usual manner of raccoon families the first winter. But perhaps she would acquire a family of her own when spring came 'round again. She was a sturdy female, the sort on which the species depends for survival.

In this respect our hopes were rewarded, for early the following summer we began watching her tree closely and were on hand to see four bright-eyed kits being led from the den by their intrepid mother, who now began the whole cycle over again—teaching her children all that she had learned from *her* own mother twelve short months before.

OPPOSITE / *She tried many dens*

THREE

The Raccoons Who Came to Dinner

Flora and her children and grandchildren thrived in our valley and came almost every evening to eat on our back porch. With so many raccoons all around us, it is not surprising that I turned to my typewriter to tell the story of my first pet raccoon, Rascal, who became the hero of my memoir by that name.

The book is called *Fripon* in the French edition, *Rascal, der Waschbär* in the German translation, and *My Rascal Far-off* in the Japanese version. From these countries and many others, letters began to pour in. American conservationists and naturalists such as Joseph Wood Krutch and Edwin Way Teale found the book interesting, as did schoolchildren and adults everywhere.

The most rewarding letters came from correspondents who had been feeding and observing raccoons for many years. Some were from nearby neighbors here in New Jersey; many others were from the Pacific Coast. The raccoon lore these letters contain seems to me so fascinating that I am passing some of it along in this and the next chapter.

Harriett E. Weaver might be cited as a typical example of these raccoon admirers. Her furry friends are denizens of the Sierra and the Coast redwood forests, and Harriett herself was for twenty years the only uniformed woman in the California State Park Service. She was on duty with the ranger crews of the state's largest redwood parks, and part of the time served as Park Naturalist. Miss Weaver is at work on what promises to be a fascinating book concerning those twenty years. She has already published an excellent volume on the redwoods entitled *There Stand the Giants*.

Harriett helped scores of forest orphans get a start in life. Among her young raccoons, one named Frosty stayed with her for many months. But in general she believes as I do that when any wild creature is ready for its freedom it should be freed. It is far better to meet animals on what might be called an equal basis, and in their own environment.

One of her happy duties was to conduct the evening campfires where hundreds gathered beneath the enormous trees to listen to her stories. Often as she was speaking, another bright-eyed audience moved into the firelight, possibly more interested in the cookies and candy bars than in the evening's nature narrative.

"During my twenty summers at Big Basin, my life was one continuous round of raccoons," Harriett says.

"The raccoons were very intelligent. They knew that the park was not only a preserve for massive and majestic trees. They had concluded that *they* deserved equal protection, and that this forest

OPPOSITE / *Harriett Weaver and Frosty*

belonged to them personally. Human beings were little more than uninvited guests owing them a continuous meal ticket.

"For more than half a century the evening routine has been the same. Vacationers bring their Coleman lanterns to the gathering place. Then they beat on pots and pans with their big cooking spoons—sounds which echo strangely through the forest. All is quiet for a few minutes after this dinner bell has been rung. Then through the huckleberry bushes and from behind the giant trees dozens of little lights appear, as bright as live coals in the shadows. To me this was always the magic hour, when raccoon families and human families eagerly awaited each other in the glow of the lanterns and the warmth of the campfires.

"The happy shouts of the children never frightened the raccoons as the furry ones moved confidently toward the circle of campers. With irresistible charm, they sat up expectantly, ready to catch any delicacy tossed their way. Since raccoons reproduce at an early age, some of the veteran vacationers who brought their children and grandchildren may have fed fifteen or twenty generations of these hungry rascals.

"All of this was enjoyed by the rangers too, but with modifications. We knew that the campfire charmers, wheedling cream puffs, Eskimo Pies and angel's food cake, were little opportunists who preferred the campers for only one reason—the exotic fare. That sort of luxury wasn't ranger food. We needed a more substantial diet to sustain us through ten to sixteen working hours each day.

"But we had the comfortable assurance that when the tourist season was over, the raccoons would remember us once again. If you can't get cake you soon learn where to get bread. On the very day the campers left, and while the rangers were putting away the big green garbage cans for winter repair and storage, the raccoons would begin to appear at our back doors, mildly contrite and obviously begging. We might not have the delicious tidbits to which they had become accustomed, but we did have food. All winter and spring, and right up to the next camping season, they gave us their undivided attention."

Harriett Weaver writes that the Big Basin raccoons are like seacoast and other raccoons in their ability to change their sleeping and waking habits. Any raccoon would rather eat than sleep if the weather is even relatively pleasant, and they never miss an invitation to breakfast, lunch or dinner if they can possibly accept.

"In our rather moderate climate," she says, "raccoons do not hibernate. In fact they do not really hibernate anywhere. Here in California they may sleep away a cold or rainy spell. But during the winter at Big Basin they were usually around day or night. We often heard them in their home under our floor, bumping their heads on the water pipes. In this off-season they wandered the park—as they never did when the campers were with us—quite aware that they now dominated the great, dark, redwood forest. They were a comfort to us, companionship in a lonely woods. We loved their cheerful company. They could now prowl Park Center and enjoy any warmth of the sun slanting down through the age-old trees.

"There were usually from seventeen to twenty raccoons in 'the gang' and they stayed together. My friend Ethel and I would see them outside, poking through the redwood duff, searching for insects and grubs. Whenever we had a treat which we knew would be appealing, we rapped on the window and they came flying. In a matter of seconds, 'the gang' would rush for the house and swarm up the steps of the back porch in an undulating mass of luxurious fur and then rumble into the kitchen.

"Even without such an invitation they were promptly on hand for dinner every evening. November and December are chilly at Big Basin, so Ethel and I would sit at the table wearing warm, heavy jackets, with collars turned up. Closing the kitchen door would have been inhospitable and unthinkable. It would have shut out our friends the raccoons—always welcome guests at our cabin."

No raccoon is identical to any other raccoon, as raccoon-watchers know. Harriett Weaver considers them at least as individual and eccentric as human beings—each animal a distinct and sometimes difficult personality.

"Besides their identifying nicks and scars, and their varied mannerisms and tones of voice, they revealed differences in maturity since they ranged in age from a few months to perhaps ten years. The old and philosophical raccoons took their food calmly, their soft hands lingering in ours. The young snatched everything until they learned that we could be trusted. Ethel and I knew them all by sight and sound, and each had an appropriate name.

"I particularly remember two greatly contrasting characters named Gramp and Smarty. Young Smarty was a brash and utterly incorrigible juvenile delinquent who would challenge any raccoon who made the mistake of crossing his path. Although the smallest and youngest of the group, he did not hesitate to tackle battle-scarred old-timers five times his size and ten times his age.

"Gramp was old and wise and gently devious. As a matter of fact he got away with more than Smarty ever could, because he was so smooth about it. He would let the whole furry mob pour into the kitchen ahead of him to accept our handouts. He remained modestly in the background beside the door because he was the only one who had discovered that just behind the door was our carton of English walnuts. While the rest of the crowd sat up for crusts of bread, he kept his eyes as rigidly front and center as a West Point cadet. But all of this time he was reaching ever so slyly around the door and into the box to get himself a special treat. This went on for weeks until all the nuts were gone. Ethel and I and Gramp were the only ones who ever knew the walnuts had been there."

Harriett Weaver is by no means the only raccoon-feeder in California. Raccoons are plentiful throughout the well-watered parts of the state and they even appear in the semi-desert areas. *Procyon lotor pallidus,* one of the recognized subspecies, inhabits the dry parts of California, Nevada, Utah and New Mexico. His pallid color apparently helps to protect him from the sun. The much more prevalent subspecies in California is *Procyon lotor psora,* common to the redwood country, and *Procyon lotor pacificus,* which prefers northern California, Oregon and Washington.

But by whatever scientific name, raccoons seldom climb above the six-thousand-foot level and that is one reason why the experiences of the naturalist Harry James are so unusual. He lives above six thousand feet in the San Jacinto Mountains and expected to find no raccoons when he moved to his big log cabin amid the evergreens beside a little spring whose overflow he had directed into an attractive pond. From somewhere came frogs, and then raccoons to catch the frogs. He put table scraps on his feeding rock beside the pool and in time lured foxes, coyotes, skunks, bobcats and even a rare mountain lion or two. Being an excellent photographer as well as a very effective conservationist, he was soon happily preoccupied clicking his shutter. Some of his shots would be hard to duplicate, particularly the one at the hummingbird feeder and the classic of the raccoon chasing away the coyote.

As all of us who are "beast watchers" know, it takes many years of close observation to discover all the characteristics and peculiari-

Waiting for Harry to serve dinner ON OPPOSITE PAGE / *a raccoon sipping sugar water from the hummingbird feeder*

ties of the various animals. Raccoons in particular continue to surprise even the most experienced observers. Mr. James writes:

"In short order the raccoons took over the rock, the pond and the family as well. One summer evening a group of nine suddenly appeared on the rock to see what hors d'oeuvres might be available. Within a matter of weeks they were showing a keen interest in everything that went on inside the house. Two of them acquired the habit of sitting on a table that was conveniently located on the porch just outside the living room window. They liked to see what we were doing, but were even more fascinated by television."

Who's afraid . . . . .

TV watching, incidentally, has been reported by many other reliable correspondents. Several raccoons, including the remarkable Tinker, hero of a later chapter, shift stations, possibly for the fun of twisting the dial. There is, however, a genuine interest in what the raccoon is hearing and seeing. The Forrestal Laboratory, after an exhaustive study, says the raccoon has the keenest sense of hearing of any mammal they have tested. Color television does not increase raccoon concentration, since *Procyon lotor* is color-blind. But he does prefer plenty of action and harmonious music. And his binocular vision and sensitive ears make him an avid TV fan.

Geri and Mike Mordkin, who live in a beautiful part of northwestern New Jersey not far from the Delaware Water Gap, have been playing host to a pair of raccoons since they first came for a handout in 1961. They named the male Misha and the female Grisha after the beloved Russian clowns.

. . . . . *of a little wolf?*

Mike Mordkin is a son of the famous dancer and choreographer Mikhail Mordkin, who danced with Pavlova. It is little wonder that the television set is frequently turned to a program of ballet, or that the graceful figures, moving across the screen like a flight of birds, hold Misha's undivided attention.

The raccoons often appeared for dinner and an evening's entertainment. But recently, when the Mordkins were adding a wing to their house, Misha decided to move in permanently. Leonard Lee Rue, a meticulous naturalist and gifted photographer, was invited to watch and photograph Misha. Leonard, author of *The World of the Raccoon* and *The World of the White Tail Deer*, has furnished numerous photographs for the book you are now reading. He took the amusing sequence of Misha watching TV.

We ourselves have our home in an equally wooded and raccoon-haunted region. Directly across the road from us in Primrose Valley live Edgar and Joyce Anderson, wood-carvers and designers of the interiors of several distinguished modern churches. The Andersons, who are hi-fi enthusiasts, discovered several years ago that music entrances raccoons.

One old male seems particularly addicted to Bach and Beethoven, and has specific preferences among the recordings. One

Misha likes television; sucks his paw

*his is getting
exciting*

*Commercials
bore me*

*hink I'll take
a nap*

evening when we were visiting the Andersons they assured us that this gentle old raccoon almost always arrived within a few minutes after they started playing Beethoven's Ninth. My pet raccoon Rascal had had his preferences too, but nothing quite so classic.

We were frankly somewhat skeptical as "Shorty" Anderson, a very sensible, six-foot-four-inch ex-Army Engineer, put on the LP record of the Boston Symphony's rebroadcast from Tanglewood. However as the questing, restless, mysterious first movement of Beethoven's greatest symphony drifted out through the forest on that summer night, my skepticism vanished. There was the sound of a screen door being opened by the old raccoon, who had come to sit before the speaker of the hi-fi cabinet. And when the majestic music had surged to its close, he quietly pushed open the screen door and went softly back to his home in the forest.

Sensitive raccoons, needing food, entertainment and affection, seem to live in every part of the United States. And with remarkable discernment they discover human beings willing to purvey these pleasures.

Miss Nora Evans, who lives in Mill Valley in the San Francisco Bay area, is an unusual woman who should publish a full account of her experiences. At seventy-nine she has just completed her twenty-eighth pack trip with the Sierra Club, hiking through two of the passes which are above twelve thousand feet. She was a debutante some sixty years ago, then taught school for forty-one years, before retiring at the age of sixty-three "to have fun." She took up surfboarding in her mid-sixties and rode her first elephant and her first ostrich on a world tour in her mid-seventies. Ever since "retirement" she has been cooking gourmet dinners for her many friends, both human and raccoon.

"The raccoons started raiding my garbage can in 1949," Nora writes. "I was determined to make a closer acquaintanceship with these little visitors. One evening a mother raccoon and her twins approached my back steps. They did not run when they saw me but began hesitantly edging toward me. I went into the kitchen and returned with a handful of grapes.

"One of the babies held back, so I named it Timid. The other little raccoon came bravely forward with its mother, so I christened it Courageous.

"After this first meal of grapes, Courageous came alone on subsequent evenings to eat from my hand. Soon she was eager to enter the kitchen, and probably would have crawled into the refrigerator if I had let her. But her hours were irregular and sometimes I missed her visit.

"This gave me an inspiration. I hung an ornamental brass bell on the back porch. To this I attached a bell cord with a pinch clothespin at the lower end. I baited the clothespin with white chicken meat, a delicacy Courageous always enjoyed. Then with excitement I waited inside the house.

"Sure enough, just as dusk was descending I heard the bell. Looking out I saw my brave young friend nibbling on the chicken and, of course, ringing the bell. Quietly I opened the door and invited her into the house for a beaten egg and a ripe persimmon— two of her favorite dishes.

"After that, for about ten nights, I continued to bait the cord, and each evening heard the bell as Courageous reached for her food.

"Then, one night, I decided to see whether she was intelligent enough to ring the bell without the bait. Dusk came—then dark —but no Courageous. I had two friends as guests that evening. We

Nora Evans and a guest. ON THE FOLLOWING PAGES / *Courageous*
reaches for the bell rope, then rings the dinner gong

were in the dining room eating our dessert when one of my visitors said, 'Someone is at the kitchen door. I hear a bell ringing.'

"We hurried to the kitchen, and there on the back porch was
Courageous waiting for her meal. Despite the presence of two
people unknown to the raccoon, she came boldly in and ate her

From her best Majolica tureen

dinner. My friends could scarcely credit what they were seeing. After that I never had to bait the bell cord again.

"One evening when the little raccoon and I were alone in the kitchen, I showed her a raw egg and said, 'If you want this, go outside and ring the bell.' She reached for the egg several times with her dainty hands, but I held it away from her and said:

" 'Don't you understand English? If you want this egg go outside and ring the bell.'

"I could hardly believe it, but she went to the back porch, rang the bell and returned for her reward—the egg. To make certain that she had mastered the trick I repeated my demand on many later evenings. Holding out tidbits such as candy, grapes or fruitcake I would say, 'I want you to go ring the bell.' She never failed to do so, and in time would ring the bell on command, even without a reward.

"It was merely speculation when I called Courageous 'she.' But when two years later I answered the bell one evening, there was my favorite raccoon with a furry baby on each side.

"Fortunately one of my best friends is Jessie Smith, a prize-winning photographer who often watched this little trio arrive and saw how the mother taught her children to ring the bell. Jessie has made many excellent photographs of the raccoons during the last sixteen years, as one generation after another passed along the art of ringing the dinner gong. I never had to teach a raccoon again. They have simply taught each other for at least ten generations."

All along the Pacific Coast, from San Francisco Bay to Puget Sound, western hospitality helps to reaffirm one's faith in humankind. At many gracious homes the raccoons who come to dinner are fed almost as well as the human guests.

Sylvia Summerland, who has a charming apartment in Seattle, with a large second-floor terrace overlooking Puget Sound, entertains her black-masked, furry neighbors for months on end. She and her mother, who lives in the adjoining apartment, have spoiled the raccoons with every sort of delicacy—green grapes in season, 100% Krinko Wheat Bread, salted wafers and parts of every roast or broiled fowl that comes from the kitchen. Word of such a raccoon restaurant gets around.

Miss Summerland holds a well-paid position with Pacific Northwest Bell. When a mother raccoon and two kits climbed to her balcony one afternoon a few years ago she saw no reason for not giving them her best, never imagining that in time they and their offspring and friends would make a discernible dent in her income. When autumn winds grow cool, and raccoons really begin to eat, as we have said, it is not unusual for a single animal to devour three or four pounds of food a day. Multiply this by thirteen, the number of raccoons Sylvia is now feeding, and it is understandable why not all of the daily fare can be grapes and tender chicken meat.

As the mob grew larger, Sylvia and her mother did not always call them "the children," but sometimes "the livestock." The Summerlands continued to set as delicious a table as they could afford, however, including marshmallows for dessert.

"I like to buy marshmallows of the large gooey variety," Sylvia says, "to see our insatiable darlings pick them up with their long,

lacy fingers or even catch them out of the air in their mouths, then watch them sit up, chewing happily as the morsel sticks on one long raccoon fang after another. It is something like feeding peanut butter to a dog—a dirty trick!—but such fun! The raccoons are good-natured about it because they are simply crazy for marshmallows."

Eventually Sylvia and her mother faced the inevitable, as all raccoon-feeders must. They began buying dog food in the giant economy size. They also began to make rather frequent trips to a local bakery where they ask, with no embarrassment, for day-old loaves, "Raccoon bread please!" (Ten loaves for a dollar.) Incidentally, we do the same in Morristown, New Jersey.

Sylvia says, "If we attract any more raccoons we may have to start eating raccoon bread ourselves. But how can we deny those appealing little rascals? Every time they hear the Sarna Bells on my mother's door as she slides it open, all thirteen of them come and sit up, their arms outstretched toward us, their eyes and ears focused upon us as we look down from the balcony above. You just can't say to thirteen hungry children, 'Sorry, but there is nothing to eat today!'"

Miss Summerland's apartment overlooks a grassy ravine. Beyond are many lovely homes with swimming pools and wide lawns and flower gardens. The raccoons sometimes swim in the pools or come to dabble in the big pan of water that Sylvia and her mother keep clean and fresh on the grass below the balcony. The baby raccoons like to carry a few pebbles to the pan and then fish for them. But they also muddy the water with their wading and sometimes tip the pan over. It is a good thing that while the daughter is at work earning raccoon food, her mother is at home to tend to the pan of water and afternoon snacks for the little dabblers.

"Seattle has many wonderful parks," Sylvia writes in a recent letter. "One is located very near our apartment. Queen Anne Hill was at one time the jewel case that housed the wealthy pioneer families of our city, and this particular park was named for one of these pioneers—a man named Kinnear. The natural woods have been left intact. There are paths, tennis courts, view-gazing places, rendezvous for lovers, benches for the elderly and swings for the young. It is here too that the raccoons make their safe home, but we have never found their den trees. They are not in the least afraid of the children in the park, or on our balcony."

It is easier to love one person than all of mankind; easier to forgive, to understand and to minister to daily needs. This is also true of our affection for a pet. We don't love all dogs and all cats and all raccoons. We usually find a particular individual. Those who are lonely seek others who are lonely; the need is mutual.

I found such an individual in *my* pet raccoon, Rascal. I was eleven, and my brilliant mother had been dead for four years. My brother was away at war. My older sisters were living their own lives. My father was often away from home on business. But in that big empty house in southern Wisconsin I had a little raccoon who slept with me, ate with me, swam, fished and climbed trees with me. When he went away to live in the woods, I was bereft.

Sylvia Summerland has apparently had a similar experience. Among the many raccoons that came to her balcony there was a young male she calls The Loner. Sometimes he limped a little and was a laggard as the other raccoons rushed in to feed. But he also stayed behind after they were gone, and soon could be petted lightly and gently on his back and head.

"As autumn progressed into winter he remained a little longer, that much closer to us because he was often the only raccoon on the balcony. Without the competition of the other raccoons he became more poised, grew larger and seemed more anxious to receive the human touch.

"On a memorable day he reached around the edge of the sliding door and let himself into the living room. He soon learned where the 'raccoon bread' was stored, but unlike most raccoons did not steal a single slice but waited for our approval. He grew fonder and fonder of me as I grew fonder of him.

"No matter at what time of the night I might come home, sometimes two or three in the morning, there was The Loner curled in front of my door, eager for love and a snack from the kitchen. I never tried to pick him up, simply gave him the gentle caress that seemed to mean more to him than the food. The two of us enjoyed each other's company in the solitude of those dark hours.

"But one day a Seattle newspaper, obviously desperate for news, started a tongue-in-cheek series of stories about a masked prowler who had been seen looking into windows along our street. Eventually the woman who had started the scare called in the police, thus bringing the drama to its tragic climax.

"A small boy told me where to find him—in a garbage can—my Loner with five bullets in his body—the victim of a frightened woman and a policeman with a gun.

"But among the new raccoon kits who have come to my balcony this summer, there is a shy little male who limps a little and likes to be petted. Maybe Loner the Second will wait for me when I come home late at night."

What might be called the "suburban sprawl" applies to raccoons as well as human beings. Raccoons are still to be found in many cities, from Seattle to New York and from Chicago to New Orleans, but for the better life they usually move to the suburbs.

Several years ago George Schuster and his family established themselves in a comfortable home in Berea, which is a suburb of Cleveland, Ohio. The songbirds were there before them, and Mr. Schuster decided to become a friend of the local wild life. He hung a large bird feeder near one of his windows to watch the chickadees, nuthatches, downy woodpeckers and other airborne freeloaders that sailed in from a nearby park. Birdseed was a minor item on his budget.

However, one evening a big female raccoon found the bird feeder, climbed aboard, unhooked it and emptied the contents in a matter of minutes. Mr. Schuster was startled, but also fascinated. He decided to play host to the new guests.

The first raccoon must have been talkative. The next evening she brought her offspring and a few dear friends. Within three years, more than fifty hungry raccoons were coming every evening for dinner. They didn't push, or shove, or nip. All were ladies and gentlemen. They lined up amiably as they moved toward the open window where Mr. Schuster, in all weathers, handed each raccoon one slice of bread.

Soon the harried but happy man was buying one hundred loaves of stale bread a week.

The remarkable pictures were taken by Glenn Zahn of the *Cleveland Press*. He is very partial to raccoons.

FOUR

Raccoons as Pets

It might seem a logical step (but not necessarily a wise one) to progress from raccoon-feeding to raccoon-rearing. It usually takes a very special person, one with great tolerance and a sense of humor, to get along amiably with these wild and wonderful little creatures. Raccoons are madly unpredictable, insatiably curious, bright, mischievous, exasperating and adorable. They can be affectionate, loyal and incredibly appealing, particularly while quite young. They can also be very difficult.

No one should acquire a raccoon, however, who is not prepared to care for it as one might a baby, during at least the first few weeks of its existence. Blind for its initial three weeks and bottle-fed for its first two or three months, the raccoon needs warmth, constant love and a watchful eye. A ten- or twelve-year-old child who respects the raccoon as an individual, loves it as a friend and

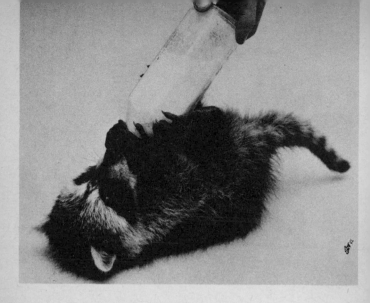

This is the way baby gets his milk . . .

protects it like a younger sister or brother is the perfect raccoon owner. He and the raccoon will both mature during a year together.

If one buys a raccoon it should always be young and healthy. Never purchase your pet from anyone but a reputable dealer or breeder. Usually, however, a raccoon comes into your life by accident. A big tree falls, revealing a den of whimpering and frightened kits, each as small as your fist. A dog or an automobile kills a nursing mother raccoon. What can you possibly do but adopt the helpless baby?

Theoretically, I suppose, even when such an orphan is left on your doorstep, you should check immediately with a game warden to see whether the laws of your state allow you to keep a pet raccoon. But since the alternative to feeding the hungry kit is, in all probability, a death sentence, the humanity of some of these laws may well be questioned. Any small raccoon turned loose before the age of three months has little chance of surviving. However, in many states it is legal to own a raccoon, and in others, exceptions will be made in such a crisis.

The immediate needs of your foundling are a substitute den, a warm meal and a well-wrapped hot water bottle. Any comfortable box placed in a dark corner will suffice at first, for if the kit is less than three weeks old and still blind he will not be able to do much climbing.

Heat about an ounce of milk to which you can add two drops of maple syrup and a drop of cod liver oil. Be sure the milk is not more than lukewarm—the temperature that would be right for a baby.

If the little raccoon is weak or sick you may need to use an eye dropper or a doll's nursing bottle. I fed my pet raccoon by taking milk in my mouth and tipping a clean wheat straw down to his eager lips. Very soon, however, Rascal was able to nurse vigorously from a full-sized baby bottle.

. . . until he can milk a cow all by himself

At first a small raccoon must be fed six times a day. After the first three or four weeks, feedings can be less frequent, but a much larger quantity of milk or formula is given at each feeding. If the raccoon is healthy and happy you will be amazed how rapidly he grows.

It is almost impossible to generalize about raccoons after they open their eyes and begin to play and climb. Some are as amenable as kittens; some are little devils. Some have fairly good table manners and some are quite messy. Most raccoons are easily housebroken to a box of sand or shredded newspapers, and later to brief excursions on a leash. I had no trouble whatsoever with Rascal because his den was a hollow tree in the back yard. Later, when he began sleeping with me, he learned to open the screen door, letting himself out of the house at any time of the day or night. We never had an accident, and he completely trained himself. But in this respect, too, raccoons differ.

Mrs. Saul R. Buc of Easton, Pennsylvania, one of the hundreds of raccoon owners who have written me, tells vividly of the first few weeks with her engaging and demanding pet. She calls her raccoon Saucy, for a justifiable reason.

"We once had an organized household, but now we have an enchanting baby raccoon.

"Mother is visiting, so that one or the other of us can raccoon-sit all day long, if only for sheer joy. 'Come see what Saucy is doing now!' means dropping everything in the way of household tasks and rushing to the living room. It is usually to find this small bundle of personality stalking our miniature poodle, Cindy, or fingering delicately, but never breaking, a translucent teacup or Dresden figure.

"Saucy is a little girl, which may explain her delicacy. She spent her first three days in a parakeet cage which she promptly outgrew, because she more than doubled in size in two weeks. You would think she was a real human baby except that she develops at about ten times the human rate. I tied a knot in an old woolen sock to give her something to play with. It is hung at a convenient height. Saucy climbs it, stalks it, battles it, lies on her back and paddles it, and from the confiding notes we hear, loves it as a dear friend and den-mate. Woolworth's toy counter has added other friends and companions such as a rattle which she shakes continuously, and a stuffed dog with which she sleeps as any child might do.

"We are surprised at the great range of her vocabulary. I imagine baby raccoons are called 'kits' because they actually purr. Her little soft whistle is about the sweetest woodland note I have ever heard, and she reserves it for me. If I have been away from her for even so much as an hour she makes that birdlike whistling coo as soon as she hears my voice. But it is fortunate I cannot translate her profanity when I am late with her food, her bath or her daily walk.

"Most of the house is not only neat and clean, but rather distinguished. But we have an open bookcase in the kitchen which is something of a glory hole. It has a curtain across it to hide cookbooks, purses, work gloves and other lares and penates. It is Saucy's particular heaven, and she rummages by the hour. Here she plays hide-and-seek and many other games of her own invention. Old riding boots are wonderful places to hide. Sometimes we can pull her out with no opposition and sometimes she fights valiantly for her new den, never biting, but hanging on with all four feet and telling us plainly that we have invaded her private castle.

"All little raccoons need a den, a dark and safe place to hide in. I tie an old sweater around my neck with the hammock effect in front like a wrong-way basket for a papoose. Saucy purrs happily in this perambulating cradle while I do my housework, wash the dishes and use the vacuum sweeper. Meanwhile, my little poodle

drops his eyes and whimpers because he isn't getting similar attention.

"Saucy loves a good head of hair. My mother has a great heap of gleaming auburn hair which she wears swept up, and held in place by combs. Between the combs and the earrings, Saucy goes berserk, ecstatic with pleasure. My hair is shorter and not so much fun, but my glasses delight her, and my whole face gets a marvelously sensitive exploration with those little black hands. I am probably the only person alive who has to wash raccoon prints from my reading glasses. When frightened, she retreats into the 'den' of the wrong-way sweater, trembling against me and asking for protection.

"No hour I have spent in watching her is ill-spent. One day she discovered her back feet, and just like a human baby spent hours playing with them. Smack on her back she watched them, put them into her mouth and chattered at them. If we could only keep her this age forever.

"Her efforts to get off the kitchen linoleum tickle us. Nothing in her ancestry could have prepared her for anything so shiny and slippery. She tries to run to the edge as swiftly as possible, but often goes down in an ignominious spraddle. Here, or on the grass beyond the door, instinct prompts her to clutch the nearest foot and climb. Such churring, crooning and tender gratitude when she is once again safely in our arms.

"I am buying her a gold collar with a leash, and will soon take her crayfishing. But, as with children, we worry about the days to come, her adolescence and young maturity. Will she still love us at first mating time as she does today?"

The change which eventually transforms the developing raccoon is undoubtedly glandular, and we who are adults should treat it with at least as much tolerance as we show toward young human beings entering the same difficult phase. Too much tolerance, however, can be a major mistake.

How rapidly a charming, trustworthy pet can become a teen-age brat was demonstrated to us recently by a raccoon named Miss Rascal, owned by our friends the Schultzes. Norman is a retired banker. Jane is a talented painter. Together with their three boys they raise deep-voiced, prize-winning bloodhounds, who look just as sad and speak just as dolefully after winning Best of Show as they would if they had lost every ribbon.

To be certain that life remains exciting around the house, this family also has a spider monkey, two female Siamese cats and their many kittens. Trying to carry on a conversation while these lovely but mischievous characters clamber over one is a feat of special concentration, but Norman and Jane manage it beautifully. They are good raconteurs.

On the afternoon when we first met Miss Rascal she was about nine months old and a complete love. She came to me when I trilled to her in raccoon language, climbed all over me, smelled me, chewed lightly upon my fingers, ears and nose and then examined my head and face as carefully as would a phrenologist or a sculptor. Feeling the gentle hands of a raccoon upon your face is a rare experience. It is as though a blind person were seeking to understand your character through fingertips alone. Miss Rascal decided within minutes that I was a raccoon-lover, or perhaps just another raccoon. Every action showed that she was exceptionally intelligent. But she wasn't always gracious, we were told. She had intense preferences, as do many raccoons. She distinctly disliked the spider monkey, but frolicked happily with the cats, the kittens and the bloodhounds.

We were immediately aware that she reacted instantaneously to varying tones of voice. Reprimanded for playing with a fragile bit of statuary, she put back her ears and hissed. Complimented for obeying the command, she began to purr. She already knew her name and would come for food when called. She understood a few other words, but just how many was still a question.

Like most raccoons she could open the icebox to get herself a snack, but she had not yet learned the common raccoon trick of turning on faucets.

"She's restless because she wants her shower," Jane said.

At the word "shower," Miss Rascal pricked up her ears and again began to purr.

What happened next was interesting. I said in a matter-of-fact tone of voice:

"What's the matter with your little pet? Many raccoons turn on their own shower."

Miss Rascal did not react for about thirty seconds. Then she rippled up the open stairway at a gallop and a few moments later we heard the scratching and scrambling of a raccoon climbing to a bathroom window sill beside the open shower. Next the mixer went on and there was more commotion and splashing. A few minutes later (and without turning off the shower) a very wet and happy raccoon came dripping back to the living room, purring, churring and telling us quite plainly that she was as bright as any raccoon in New Jersey.

One month later this doll had become a vixen. Knowing I had found a very special raccoon I came back with Guy Gillette, the well-known *New York Times* photographer.

"I don't understand it," Jane said. "Miss Rascal has become an absolute devil in the last two weeks. She rips furniture, hisses at the cats and dogs and tries to kill the spider monkey. We have had to lock her in one of our big dog runs. She's bitten Norman several times."

"She won't bite me," I said. "She loves me."

"That's what you think," Norman said.

Guy looked a little nervous about coming into the large enclosure with me. But since he can get a good picture at a distance of ten feet while I needed to be within inches of the raccoon, he was relatively philosophical about our venture.

The little character who had been so loving on the previous occasion came snarling out of her nest box and wasn't soothed by any of my tender coaxing. I extended a juicy tidbit but she preferred my finger.

"It's nothing," I assured my wife and Jane. "But could you bring me a little iodine and a pair of gloves?" Then my ex-friend Miss Rascal and I posed for several pictures, with Guy clicking the shutter at a safe distance.

Young raccoons, like growing children, are interesting because their minds are developing. Curiosity is at the root of all learning. But it is also at the root of much mischief. Gordon Blandford's twin raccoons, Candy and Chucky, entertained and instructed us all through the summer of 1965.

Reverend Blandford was born of Russian parents in Manchuria and in his extreme youth was one of the desperately hungry waifs who became legend after World War I. Adopted by an American couple who were Seventh Day Adventist missionaries, he assumed their surname and their religion. In time he became a missionary himself, and also an expert on the moths and butterflies of America and Asia, assembling several fabulous collections, some now in museums.

When the Seventh Day Adventists purchased a large wooded tract below us on Primrose Brook, we were disturbed by only one eventuality. In grading and leveling the land for a parsonage and a church, they wiped out the best crayfishing area along the stream. Some twenty raccoons depended upon a very shallow lake and marsh on that property, located just above an ancient and crumbling dam. The Adventists converted part of this area to a baptismal pool, but the raccoons felt they had been ousted. Over a period of weeks more than fifteen were hit by cars on an adjoining highway.

Came the Blandfords, and much exchange of knowledge on moths, butterflies and even raccoons, which they had reared and studied in Taiwan and Massachusetts. They had no raccoons when they arrived but were anxious to acquire a pair. By ironical coincidence, as Reverend Blandford motored to a second sermon on a Saturday in May, a huge den tree fell on the road just missing his car, and from a large hollow limb tumbled twin three-day-old raccoons, soon named Candy and Chucky. All summer we watched, studied and photographed them.

One might think that two raccoons, found on a Saturday and raised not only in a parsonage but in the Elder's study would be exceptionally good little animals. Once in a while they were. But by the time Candy had only one eye open, she pounced on Chucky's tail. She never for a moment lost her advantage over her shy and gentle brother. She was the leader in all the mischief as the weeks went by. She raided Gordon's desk and scattered his sermons. She showed Chucky how to lift the lid on the tropical fish tank where they both dined on some very fancy fantail mollies, red swordtails, neons and guppies. It was Candy who knocked down a framed display of special moths. Each knew his name, would come when called and learned to ring the doorbell when tired of wandering in the woods.

I was particularly anxious to see how early this pair of raccoons would learn to manipulate faucets. Every day they watched Gor-

*First
the twins
turn on
the faucet*

*Then
they get
a cool drink
and also
a bath*

Then they go swimming in the baptismal pool

don or his wife turn on the outside faucet which provided them with a hose to play with.

One afternoon Gordon phoned with excitement and asked us to hurry over. We were lucky to be present on the very day they were big enough and bright enough to turn it on for themselves.

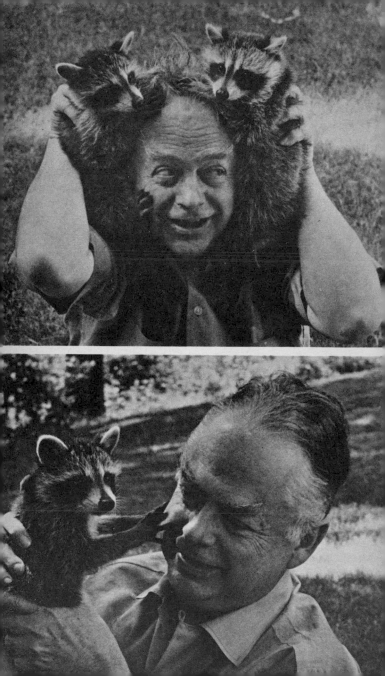

The author and the raccoons

They were not quite three months old. My talented son-in-law Clarence E. Olson took the pictures of the event, and of the author of this book playing with the twin raccoons.

Other neighbors of ours, Ted and Olivia Smith, have a young raccoon they named Cooney (later changed to Rosemary Cooney because she sings so much of the time and plays very bad ukelele).

Rosemary was a gift from a boy friend of one of their two college-age daughters. This boy takes his charming girl on dates in Florida where they are both going to school. His idea of a really interesting date is to catch rattlesnakes with his beloved in the Everglades, or to visit any zoo within one hundred miles. Miss Smith likes all this quite as much as the boy does. When they found a raccoon baby, however, they knew they couldn't keep it on campus, so naturally they air-expressed it to Ted and Olivia.

Ted Smith is an excellent architect, so constantly occupied with commissions that he works long hours at his office. Olivia manages their big home and estate, plus a plethora of cats and dogs. During vacations she entertains many college-age friends of the two daughters. The Smiths lead a very busy life and, like all the rest of us, experience moments of weariness.

It was not with complete delight, therefore, that they received the air-express crate containing a tiny, blonde, female and squalling raccoon. The little thing had fleas, which were soon dispatched with a safe and mild flea powder.

Olivia furnished the baby a warm, dark box on the second floor of the three-story mansion. The dogs were relegated to the first floor, the cats to the third and the mob of visiting college students to such other bedrooms as were not being used by cats, dogs and raccoons.

A raccoon learns in a very few weeks that it can be the *enfant terrible* of any household. As soon as Cooney learned to climb stairs she managed to evict the cats and the dogs, and she knew instinctively when breakfast, lunch, cocktails (with snacks) and dinner were being served. She ate on each such occasion and also in between.

Runs and kennels were soon provided for the dogs. Cat houses were built for the cats. After all, anyone named Rosemary Cooney obviously needed the entire house, the whole back yard and many acres besides.

Rosemary Cooney spent a happy summer playing in her special fountain, hiding in the nearby thickets, sitting in the crotches of the big trees, sunning and crooning to herself. Then the Smiths called us for advice. Cool weather was approaching and where could Rosemary spend the winter? They had read *Rascal* and they knew that they must provide a special and attractive den where such a guest from the wilderness could dream away the colder months. I suggested following my time-tested device of cutting a four-inch hole in the side of the garage leading to a snug bedroom inside the building. Ted, the architect, rose immediately to this creative challenge. He would make it a five-room apartment along strictly Frank Lloyd Wright lines (which, he explained, is really not *modern,* but *romantic,* and dark enough for even a raccoon).

But the best-laid plans of mice and men (to coin a phrase)! Rosemary Cooney slept in the bathroom and used the big bedroom for reverse purposes. Furthermore, in a few weeks she ran away. The Smiths wandered the woods trying to find their pet, the little blonde who tried her best to sing.

We called one day to console our friends, and Ted came beaming to the door. He said he was taking the day off to celebrate.

"Celebrate what?"

"Rosemary Cooney came home. I go out every half hour to talk with her."

"Is she living in your fabulous raccoon apartment?"

"She won't have a thing to do with it. She lives in an old box on a shelf in the garage, and she alternately beats up and then loves up her stuffed monkey."

"Does she still croon?"

"She not only croons, she plays the ukelele."

"No kidding, Ted?"

"No kidding. We gave her one of the girls' old ukes, and she holds it down firmly and plucks it."

We went out to the back yard, and there, sure enough, was Rosemary singing very badly and doing even worse on the ukelele, which she held with one front paw and plucked with the other, while gazing dreamily toward the far horizon, lost in reverie.

In crossing the country along a diagonal from the Florida keys to the Pacific Northwest one finds extreme variations in raccoon types. Among Florida's six subspecies is a diminutive, light-colored variety which seldom weighs more than five or six pounds at maturity. These fey creatures, like the tiny deer of the keys, were made for a Lilliputian world. By contrast, the raccoons of the Pacific Northwest are among the largest, darkest and most deeply furred animals of the entire breed, commonly six or seven times the weight of their little Florida cousins. Like the great trees on the well-watered and fertile western slopes of the mountains, they seem of appropriate size for the ultimate Paul Bunyan country.

Wayne Adkins is an assistant power-saw foreman (bull buck) on Weyerhaeuser's Vail-McDonald Tree Farm in western Washington. A rugged, out-of-doors man, he spends his working hours supervising the labor of loggers like his friends Kindell and Thayer, who man big power saws felling the enormous conifers. Part of his leisure time in the past was spent hunting cougars, bobcats and raccoons. But a small handful of wailing fur made a great change in his life in the month of May 1963. The tiny creature also changed the lives of his wife and four children.

On a pleasant afternoon when sunlight was slanting in through the big trees, Wayne Adkins directed his loggers to put their saw to the base of a giant cedar, showing where he wanted it felled. The motor sputtered, then roared, and the sharp teeth began to cut the fragrant wood. Soon after, with a cry of "timber," all three men leaped to safety as the monarch of the forest crashed to the ground.

A wail more disturbing than that of the saw now filled the air. It was not like anything the three men had ever heard before.

"Baby bobcats," said Forest Thayer.

"Baby cougars," said Edward Kindell.

"Might be raccoons," said Wayne Adkins. And he was right.

All three men ran back to the stump of the cedar tree where they found two tiny raccoons squalling in terror. Their eyes were not yet open, so they scarcely needed their black masks. Nor did they look like very dangerous bandits to any of the men.

Forest Thayer picked up one furry infant and Wayne Adkins the other. All three men exchanged uneasy glances. These raccoon kits would certainly die without their mother. And so began the futile search.

Kindell was sympathetic, but he didn't want either of the orphans. Thayer took one and so did Adkins. Wayne would never have believed that the little raccoon in his big hand would soon have the whole Adkins family in the palm of *his* little black paw.

It was quitting time in any case, so the three started back to the village of Doty, and Forest and Wayne told their wives similar stories. Wayne ended, "This little guy seems to need a home."

One year later the Adkins family, plus all their established pets, recognized that Tinker was now master of the household. In the pictures which follow you will see Adkins at work in the woods, son Jim, son John and daughter Penny playing with Tinker, and Mrs. Adkins taking Tinker on a shopping trip where the raccoon always wants to drink from the water fountain, turning the faucet with a back foot. Tinker doesn't relish raw meat or fish, but he loves crisp bacon and delicately scrambled eggs. In the picture which shows Mrs. Adkins on the sofa, he is kissing her in gratitude for a well-prepared meal.

Tinker romps with the terrier, Puggy, and two black puppies, races over the housetops with the Siamese cat and seems to snub no animal or human except his twin who lives in equal comfort across the street with the Thayers. He can open the icebox, switch programs when daughter Starla is watching television, and prefers to sleep with John, his special friend. John believes that Tinker has twenty meaningful sounds and that he can interpret every "word" Tinker says.

As for Wayne Adkins, he shares each meal including his morning coffee with the rascal they have adopted.

Says this rugged ex-hunter, "I can't see myself ever again shooting a raccoon."

Old Jerry (1920–1942) was probably the Methuselah of the entire raccoon world. In their wild state, raccoons seldom live to be more than ten or twelve years of age, due principally to the fact that their teeth become so worn they cannot fish, hunt or defend themselves. A few pet raccoons, fed on special diets, live to be

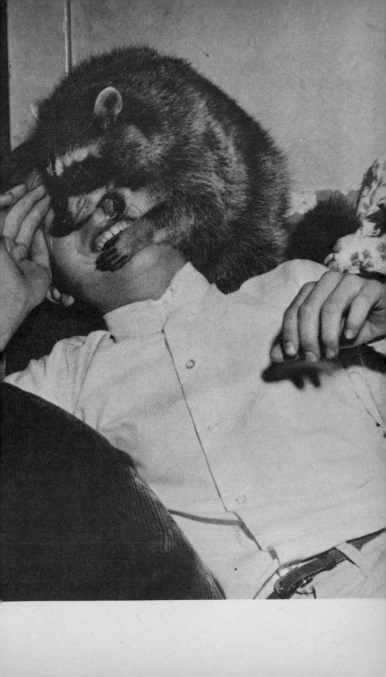

fourteen or fifteen. But Jerry outlived them all, retaining his wits, his sense of mischief and his health to a ripe old age.

Jerry's fond owners and protectors were Hazel and Bob Jones, now in their hale and hearty seventies, and happily married for over fifty years. "We have always been partners in everything," Hazel writes, "and we were partners in caring for our raccoons, foxes and little badgers. Maybe Old Jerry's long life was partly due to our love for him and the fact that every day for twenty years I baked him his favorite food, a big pan of corn bread made of coarse-ground, yellow corn meal, finely ground oatmeal with a teaspoon of soda, a pinch of salt and milk. This was cut into two-inch squares and fed with warm milk containing a few drops of good old cod liver oil. In season we gave Jerry all the sweet corn he could eat."

All the animals on the big Jones farm were more or less pets, but Old Jerry kept his proud individuality and never became completely tame. However his eyes would shine with pleasure and he would wag his tail like a dog whenever Bob or Hazel came near his big comfortable cage.

Jerry did not begin his life at the Jones place *merely* as a pet. In January 1922 when Bob and a friend named Frank were walking through Bob's woods in southern Wisconsin they saw a big, very dark and handsome raccoon sitting on the limb of a tree. Bob wanted that raccoon to mate to a female he had captured the previous year, so Frank climbed the tree to push him into the snow, and Bob after quite a struggle got him safely into a burlap sack. They calculated his age at two years.

Bob and Hazel had always loved birds and animals, and they were both delighted when the pair of raccoons produced a fine litter of kits. In another couple of years Jerry had produced, by several females, more than thirty little raccoons—too many for even this raccoon-loving family to feed and cherish. Killing and skinning the excess raccoons was wholly out of the question, even though the price of pelts was sky-high in the 1920's. So Bob hit upon the idea of selling pairs of live raccoons to other breeders.

There was a logical and humane reason for rearing raccoons in the 1920's. These attractive animals had been so ferociously over-hunted and overtrapped to satisfy the 'coonskin-coat craze that in some states they were facing extinction. It became increasingly necessary to produce new breeding stock to be released under more stringent game laws in the well-wooded areas where once they had been plentiful. Bob found a ready sale for his raccoons at thirty dollars a pair in Wisconsin, Ohio, Pennsylvania, South Dakota, Montana and California. Hazel and Bob were sad to say farewell to the raccoons they crated for shipment. But they had no choice. They were being overwhelmed each spring by beautiful litters of kits, sired by Old Jerry, now a magnificent forty-pound specimen and Sultan of a sizable harem of affectionate females.

Except for a few years during the twenties, raccoon farming has always been an unprofitable venture. Various breeders produced interesting mutations, including pure white raccoons (albinos), pure black raccoons (the melanistic phase) and various pastel shades, all of which can be genetically refined to breed true to type. But, unlike the fox and mink farmers who are still in business, the raccoon breeders faced two special disadvantages, a disastrous decline in pelt prices (and therefore in the value of breeding stock) and the undeniable fact that the voracious raccoons eat up all of the profits.

Wisconsin dairymen of that era sold most of their milk to creameries rather than to distributors. The whole milk was taken to the creamery, the cream was separated from the skim milk and the skim returned to the farmer as a nourishing food for pigs. On the Jones farm some of this skim milk went to the raccoons.

One day disaster struck. Some chemical had "accidentally" been poured into the skim milk vat. When fed to the raccoons it killed almost every animal except stout Old Jerry. Hazel and Bob were grief-stricken, and so discouraged they ceased raccoon breeding entirely. But what to do with Jerry? He was now about ten years old and his teeth were too worn to turn him out to fend for himself. They must care for him now with special tenderness, put him on a permanent pension and see that he had a happy old age. For another decade they bought the necessary state license each year so that no game warden could ever question their right to keep him.

Once Jerry escaped when a falling tree hit his cage. Knowing that he would probably die if they didn't find him, they traced him through the snow to a tree where he lay in a crotch, asleep and exhausted. Awakened by the call of his name, Jerry flashed his mischievous eyes and wagged his big ringed tail, as much as to say, "What are you doing here?" He came home peacefully, and gladly ate his fresh batch of corn bread.

Hazel writes, "One night in the autumn of 1942 he didn't answer his supper call. I looked in the nest box and there was the old fellow dead, age about twenty-two years. He had evidently died quietly and without pain—perhaps the oldest, best-fed raccoon that ever lived."

FIVE

St. Francis of Northernaire

There were two active boys who lived in southern Wisconsin half a century ago. One swam, fished and searched for pearls in Rock River. The other performed these necessary rites of boyhood in the Sugar River not far to the west. Each had a father who helped him identify the birds and animals of the region, showed him where to hunt for Indian artifacts, and took him to northern Wisconsin for a taste of "wilder wildness."

Oddly enough, I did not know my Sugar River contemporary although he lived so near me. My native Edgerton and his Monroe were small towns of a similar nature in the rolling dairy country. Elms and maples shaded the quiet streets of comfortable homes, surrounded by wide lawns and gardens. There was always plenty of space for a dog, a few cats and a coterie of other pets.

During summer vacations in northern Wisconsin our canoes

may have passed many times as we fished the beautiful chain of twenty-seven lakes from the resort village of Three Lakes where the Marty family had a cottage. In this general region Carl and I saw our first porcupines, deer, bear, osprey and eagles (long since gone from southern Wisconsin). And here we both heard for the first time the wild, haunting and spine-tingling cry of the loon.

In the early 1920's both of us published our first poetry—and still we had not met, nor even heard of each other. Carl prospered in business. I prospered more modestly in journalism and literature. But neither of us had forgotten the lost Eden of our early years. We reached vigorous middle age with a strong determination to break with routine and get back to the woods and water.

So here I am at my typewriter, looking out through a wide picture window at my little lake and waterfall in New Jersey. And there is Carl Marty at Three Lakes, Wisconsin, living intimately with more forest creatures than you will see during an entire summer canoeing through the wilderness.

Carl Marty owns and operates a charming and unusual resort called Northernaire, located on the longest interconnecting chain of inland lakes in the world. His many protected acres are near the Nicolet National Forest, which is approximately the size of Rhode Island. This has given him an opportunity to tame without imprisoning many gentle creatures. It is not unusual to see a fawn or a small bear wander into the dining room or the bar. In the well-furnished animal house, human visitors frequently see the astonishing sight of young foxes, otters, raccoons and even bears eating and romping together, and finally falling asleep in a tangle of small bodies on the davenport. Animals are free to come and go as they like since the door, and "raccoon hatch" in the floor, are usually open to the unfenced woodland beyond. Who keeps order in this ménage? It has always been an affectionate dog.

Carl's most recent quarter century might be trisected by the lifespans of three great dogs who have been his able assistants in guarding and guiding these wards. The first two dogs were cocker spaniels and the third a gallant, two-hundred-pound St. Bernard.

Rusty, a red cocker, lived from 1940 to 1948.

Rusty's golden daughter, Ginger, protected her mixed flock from 1948 to 1957.

Bernese, the huge St. Bernard, took over in 1957, and at this writing is still rescuing orphans of the storm.

Carl Marty and I agree that a dog often reflects the character and personality of the master. The hunter and his hunting dog, the shepherd and his border collie, the pampered woman and her Pekinese are good examples.

For instance, when I was a boy I had a St. Bernard almost as large as Carl's Bernese. He protected my raccoon, Rascal, Poe-the-Crow, my tame skunks, woodchucks and muskrats as well as my cats and kittens. He could have eaten any one of them in two bites, but preferred to use his enormous strength in protecting them from potential enemies, meanwhile maintaining harmony in the household. If any of the pets were too rough in their play, Wowser would speak with a deep note of authority and the contestants would meekly obey.

Each of Carl's dogs has shown similar responsibility, able to

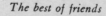

The best of friends

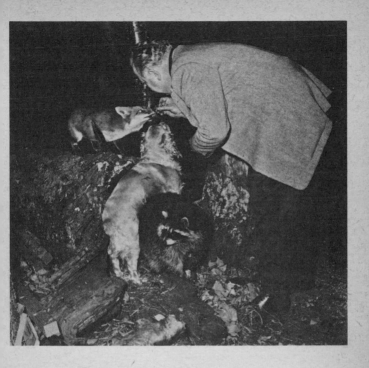

Fox, spaniel and raccoon with Carl Marty

discipline as well as guard and cherish these woodland waifs.

It was Rusty who first revealed to Carl that if a man and his dog come but ten percent of the way, the wilderness creatures will come the other ninety percent in seeking friendship.

Early in the 1940's when Carl was first developing what has since become a fabulous resort complex, he and Rusty were coming home late one evening to the family cottage where Carl lived with his wife and his son Mike. Rusty rushed ahead, whining eagerly, and as Carl rounded a bend in the path, he was amazed to see his cocker running in circles and playing happily with what appeared to be a half-grown red fox. The dog and the fox flashed in and out of the moonlight and the shadows. As Carl approached, however, the fox disappeared into the woods.

Was it possible, Carl asked himself, that a dog and a fox can be friends? Perhaps all the animals of the forest were less shy than he had imagined. Carl decided that at the first possible opportunity he would acquire a baby fox to see if this "untamable" species could be taught to trust both dog and man.

His first bright-eyed, sharp-nosed orphan was named Louie—raised by Carl on a bottle while given warmth and affection.

Even as a kit, the fox demonstrated his courage and his cunning as he played with Rusty, hid under chairs, dashed out to leap on the red cocker or disappeared like an animated phantom during games of hide-and-seek. Carl became greatly attached to this graceful, intelligent little animal.

At about seven weeks Louie started to become restless. Carl now knows that this is the exact moment, give or take a day or two, when little foxes must be released if they are ever to make return visits of their own free will. Up to this time the baby fox had nursed happily, and had then been weaned to chopped meat and cereal. He had wanted protection. But now he wished to explore beyond the confines of the cottage.

As Carl Marty explains it, "If an adolescent leaves a comfortable home, and is not held against his will, he will want to return often. But if a man is long confined in a prison cell he will want to put one thousand miles between himself and the prison."

Although this was but the first of many nursling foxes, Carl sensed the arrival of the dreaded moment of parting. He thought the woodsmen might be prophetic in saying that Louie would never again return. But when Carl asked a little girl what she thought, the child said, "Of course Louie will come back. He can't get fried chicken in the woods."

"Instead of opening the door and letting him out," Carl said, "I cut a small hole in the porch screen door. Louie was undecided. Several times he put his head through the hole, then pulled it back hastily. Finally he thrust half his body through, but again changed his mind and returned to the safe porch. Then with great determination he leapt to freedom. But panic overtook him. Once again he dashed back.

"This was an exciting new game, so Louie continued to go in and out all morning, climaxing the performance by racing around the cottage some twenty times before disappearing under the house, perhaps for a nap.

"The next time I saw Louie was two hours later. He came through the hole and onto the porch, then scratched on the living room door. We opened it for him and he made a mad dash for the papers in the kitchen where he had been trained. After a moment he looked relieved and departed through the hole in the screen.

"Every day for almost a week we had the same frantic visit from our well-trained fox before he realized that it wasn't necessary to come indoors."

Louie had now decided to be an outdoor fox with a comfortable nest under the house. Every light, soft piece of cloth he could find —mostly feminine clothing—he craftily purloined.

"Eventually Louie had half of my wife's lingerie under the cabin.

"Rusty and Louie were equally good friends outdoors or in. They chased each other in circles, often with Louie's tail in Rusty's mouth. And they often roamed the woods together.

"I would frequently astonish my guests by saying that I could produce a wild red fox in two minutes. I would call Rusty and Louie. The dog and fox would come from the woods together and put on a terrific show. But it clearly demonstrated how a fox would fight in the wild. Rusty was too slow for the fox, and Louie would jockey around so swiftly and slyly that he soon had the dog by the throat. Since this was only in fun, the fox never really closed those needle-sharp teeth, and would let Rusty escape unscathed. But it wouldn't have been that bloodless in a fight to the death.

"During the autumn, romance came into Louie's life and he set up housekeeping in the woods. We fear that he may have been trapped that winter for we never saw him again."

People ask Carl if Louie wasn't a rare phenomenon and wonder if other foxes can also be tamed. My friend at Northernaire has an excellent answer. Altogether he has raised, tamed or hand-fed more than fifty foxes, and when he gives them freedom at seven weeks, they always come back.

"One fox," Carl said, "made a practice of jumping through my open window to sleep at the foot of my bed. He always returned to the woods at daybreak. It seems to me we have somewhat changed the attitude of foxes in this area. They become tamer every year."

Carl Marty is a talented raconteur, but he reveals two characteristics rare among storytellers, modesty and regard for the truth. As you wander over the grounds of Northernaire with Carl for your guide, or walk beside him down a woodland path fragrant with pine and balsam, he may be telling you about some fawn, fox, raccoon or beaver he has recently released from "protective custody."

"Would you like to see my beaver?"

"I certainly would."

"Here, Bop, Bop, Bop! Here, Bopper!"

From a nearby cove a thirty-five-pound beaver comes swimming toward his beloved master, arises dripping from the water and takes a few dried apricots from Carl's hand. Carl frequently lies prone upon the ground to greet his friends, since, as he explains, they almost always want to touch noses, and they feel more comfortable if you are at their level. A human being, standing erect, is a formidable and frightening sight to most forest animals.

Bopper was a great favorite for all the years he lived. State trappers, using completely humane methods, were live-trapping a colony of beavers to relocate them in a more advantageous area in the nearby Nicolet National Forest. In one of the beaver lodges the men found a little beaver weighing less than one pound. He was huddled in a far corner where his mother had told him to stay—small, frightened and trembling.

The state trappers brought this diminutive animal to Carl Marty, knowing that he would be glad to take care of the orphan, and Carl gave him everything he needed—food, shelter and a "family." He was told by the trappers, however, that bringing up a baby beaver might prove an impossibility. Neither Carl nor any of the experienced woodsmen in the area had ever heard of a tiny beaver being successfully raised in captivity.

Carl often takes his smallest foundlings into his bedroom for the first few days. Young porcupines are raised in the bathtub. The little beaver slept with Carl in his bed, tucking his flat, wide tail under him so that no accident occurred. Carl read everything he could find about beavers, and found practically no helpful advice. But Carl's common sense and Bopper's rugged little physique prevailed.

At first Bopper was fed with a doll's nursing bottle, and then progressed to a regular baby bottle. Eventually he could eat bread and milk, apples and a variety of other foods. Bopper had never heard that beavers are supposed to be vegetarians, and he soon became addicted to chopped beef, choosing this first at every meal before going on to grapes, plums, prunes, apricots and dates. As he grew older and larger he liked to top his meal with the bark of a few small willow or aspen logs. On such a well-balanced diet he grew rapidly, and before he was a year old weighed more than thirty pounds.

Bopper was big and strong, but in many ways he remained a slightly spoiled and very affectionate baby. He loved to be cuddled and petted, and would come to Carl, crying to be picked up and cradled in his arms.

"If I didn't pick him up," Carl told me, "he would whimper and cry, chew the door and the woodwork, and run around like a naughty child. But if I held him in my arms, he would fall into a sound sleep in less than a minute."

Bopper the beaver wants affection

Sound asleep in less than a minute

Bopper now could cut through a good-sized branch with one snap of his strong, sharp teeth. But Carl demonstrated how safe it was to put his hand in Bopper's mouth. This very large male beaver was still as gentle as a kitten. He might hiss and lunge at another animal as a bluff, but he never attacked.

"I have never been bitten by any of my hundreds of animals," Carl said, "and I have never had one of them, not even the bears, dangerously injure any other animal in their rough play. It is a great misfortune that the human race cannot be as gallant and as gentle as are the so-called 'wild' animals."

Carl Marty believes as I do that all animals have strong, instinctive tendencies, but often learn the finer points of behavior by watching their parents at work. Before he was a year old, Bopper was given his complete freedom. He had a chain of lakes in which to swim, and hundreds of thousands of woodland acres in which to cut small trees. Now he could live the life of an independent and adult male beaver if he wanted to. But apparently his "colony" was Northernaire. So he built his lodge in a very amateurish manner beside the lake shore, near the hotel.

With no parents to guide him, however, he failed to provide an underwater entrance to this mound of brush that he called home. Carl knew that he would not be warm in such a carelessly built lodge, so he found an old trunk, lined it with clean hay, cut a hole in one end of the trunk and put this in the animal house. Bopper was very pleased with this warmer arrangement. He and two friendly muskrats slept together in that trunk for several months.

But every afternoon the beaver came to Villa Two, where Carl was now living, to relish an hour of splashing in the bathtub. He would then let out the water by pulling the plug and spend half an hour grooming and drying his fur.

Carl lets his ex-foundlings live their own lives from the moment they are prepared to fend for themselves. But he also worries about them when they are off-schedule in their visits. During the summer months Bopper had always come when called at dusk. But one Saturday night Carl waited hour after hour and no Bopper. He went to the pier and called, "Bop, Bop, Bop—here, Bopper, Bopper, Bopper!" No wet and friendly beaver came in from the lake, and Carl had nightmares of Bopper snagged on a fisherman's hook, killed by an automobile, or in some other mortal danger.

Carl could not sleep, so he read a book until far into the morning hours. Then he heard the welcome slap, slap, slap of that big

Carl, an otter and three fawns

paddle tail and went out to greet his beaver on the wharf. Something had happened, but Bopper couldn't tell him what it was. He merely cried his baby cry more plaintively, and seemed more grateful than ever when Carl picked him up and cuddled the big, wet creature in his arms.

As we continued our walk along the shore we were greeted by a dappled fawn and later by two young and playful otters. I have had a friendly relationship with many forest animals, but I have never seen anything like Carl Marty's communion with his wilderness neighbors.

"You are something like St. Francis," I said to my host.

"I wish I could live up to that compliment."

"What *is* your secret?"

"There is no secret," Carl said. "Superstitious people think that I practice some sort of mesmerism on these animals. Nothing could be farther from the truth. Most of these affectionate little fellows are my foster children who lived with me for a few days,

*Carl, baby-sitting with two fox kits, a fawn and a baby porcupine
(on the back of his neck)*

weeks or months. They looked to me for food, warmth and protection, and apparently remember me with gratitude. Unlike
human beings, who often resent a favor, these direct and simple
creatures never forget a person who has been kind."

"How many unconfined pets have you had in the last quarter
century?"

Carl stopped to think for a moment.

"It is difficult to remember exactly," he said. "But I would say
that I have had, besides Bopper, one brush wolf, six otters, seven
bears, twenty porcupines, several badgers, many skunks, more
than fifty foxes and possibly seventy-five deer."

"And raccoons?"

"At least one hundred."

"Which raccoon had the most unforgettable personality?"

Without a moment's hesitation, Carl said, "Snoopy. He was practically human."

Snoopy was the pet of a little girl who had spent her summer on the lakes. She was heartbroken that she could not take him home with her. And she made Carl Marty promise, and cross his heart, that he would take wonderful care of her raccoon when she and her parents went back to the city.

Carl, who is loved by all children as well as all animals, promised. And when Carl makes a promise he keeps it.

Introduced as an adolescent into the Marty household, the pampered but unspoiled Snoopy took over in the self-confident manner of his species. Carl called Rusty into the living room to meet his new friend. Each of Carl's dogs knows that when a wild animal tips its ears forward, it is being curious, inquisitive and willing to be convinced. When the same animal tips its ears back, it is ready to fight if necessary. Snoopy's ears were tipped forward.

The poised Snoopy watched the dog, then approached him as the cocker wagged his tail and made soothing noises. Snoopy made a churring sound that seemed very friendly. A moment later the spaniel and the well-behaved raccoon touched noses for the first time. And from that moment on they were inseparable companions.

"On the second day of their acquaintance," Carl told me, "Snoopy ventured far out on a limb over the water. Still a novice at climbing, the young raccoon slipped and fell into the lake. Rusty did not know that raccoons can swim, so he dove in and retrieved Snoopy. From then on Rusty was Snoopy's hero."

As in the case of all of Carl's pets, Snoopy had the run of the entire house. Far more curious than a cat, he examined every bureau drawer, cupboard and closet. He was not yet tall enough to manipulate the refrigerator door handle, but he was well within reach of the lower storage drawer.

"The favorite food of this particular raccoon," Carl said, "was jelly roll, which was purposely left in that accessible drawer. This initiated an exciting daily game.

"We had led Snoopy to believe that he was not to open this drawer, and it was his sly trick to try to outmaneuver us and get his jelly roll in spite of the rules.

"He would peer around the kitchen door, moving softly and silently, to see if we were watching. His bandit mask seemed very appropriate at such a time.

"If he thought we were busy reading or talking he would go cautiously to the refrigerator, ready to open the drawer. Just at this moment I would shout and slap my paper on my knee, and Snoopy would scoot behind the refrigerator knowing he had been caught in the act.

"In a few moments his beady eyes would again peer from this hiding place to see if we were still looking, and the game would go on until we would finally let him outsmart us and get his jelly roll."

Carl's Snoopy, like my raccoon Rascal, was a full-fledged member of the family. And like Rascal he was allowed to eat at the table three times a day.

"He displayed better manners," Carl said, "than many a six-year-old child, and his polite deportment amazed my friends. We kept his chair far enough back so that he could not easily climb on the table, and he would sit up expectantly, waiting for the morsels which we gave him, using his front paws in the manner of hands. He was always a delightful dinner partner.

"After dinner he usually had a good romp with his friend Rusty. They would put on a regular wrestling match, approaching each other from opposite corners of the room to meet in the center, rolling, snarling and grasping each other, all in play but with such mock seriousness that some of our uninitiated guests thought it was a dangerous fight, and pleaded with me to stop the struggle. It was easy to see how a raccoon can handle two or three dogs, for the raccoon's neck is very short, and while fighting he habitually holds his head low between his front legs while he reaches for the dog's jugular vein."

"Did Snoopy sometimes lie on his back in these contests?"

"Very frequently," Carl said, "It gave him full use of his forty sharp teeth and four well-armed paws. You've probably noticed that any full-grown raccoon is a formidable adversary. I think if the chips were down, Rusty wouldn't have had a chance."

"But haven't you discovered, Carl, that raccoons prefer to avoid a fight, and are quite amiable creatures unless forced to defend themselves?"

"It's true of raccoons," Carl said, "but also of every animal we have raised, including bears. I have yet to see *unprovoked, aggressive ferocity* in any animal, although *defensive ferocity* is fairly common. Given half a chance to be friendly, animals get along famously with other animals and also with kindly human beings.

"Dogs can be taught to trail and kill raccoons, as you know. However, it usually takes a pack to kill one raccoon, and most hounds are scarred for life after a single year of hunting. But I am convinced that these same dogs could be taught to play gently with raccoons if reared in the right manner. Man is the great predator and ruthless killer, and he can infect his dogs with the same virus."

Rusty and Snoopy were such close and constant companions that they seemed to be able to communicate their moods and intentions. One afternoon Carl witnessed an incident that opened his eyes with amazement. He didn't entirely believe it until he had seen it repeated many times. Rusty wanted to get into the house, but could not open the screen door. Carl was busy with other matters, so Rusty went to the woods and soon came back with Snoopy waddling behind him. Snoopy opened the door for his friend, and let the dog into the house. His mission accomplished, he turned and waddled back to the woods again. I can easily believe this since my raccoon, Rascal, and many others I have known, could open almost any door. How Rusty was able to make his wants known to the raccoon remains a mystery.

Some sort of communication, however, does exist among animals. All the birds in a feeding area will panic simultaneously. Was it the cry of a distant hawk, the quiet footfall of a marauding cat? No danger is in sight anywhere and yet the birds respond to what appears to have been an intercommunicated alarm. A covey of quail or grouse are so closely and sensitively related that they usually go up together without a split second intervening. Thousands of bluefish react in a similar manner when some outrider or leader of the school senses the presence of a porpoise. Bees, through elaborate dances, tell other bees exactly where to find the flowers from which they have just gathered nectar. It would be strange indeed if two such intelligent animals as Rusty and Snoopy, playing together all day and sleeping together at night, did not have some method of communication.

Carl told me that the bond between the red cocker spaniel and the very affectionate and bright raccoon was so strong that when he took Rusty for a month's trip in the autumn, the dog became so lonesome for the raccoon that he would not eat for several days. When they eventually drove back to Northernaire, Rusty's ears pricked up and he began whining eagerly. He leaped from the car and for many hours searched the forest for Snoopy. Then he came back dejected and again would not eat.

Raccoons wander in the autumn, endlessly seeking food. Snoopy had been very well fed while Carl and Rusty were gone, but he too was instinctively restless and full of wanderlust. The game warden had come across Snoopy several times two or three miles from home. The raccoon was always glad to climb into his car and ride back to the hotel for a really good meal. But on the day of the spaniel's return he was far off in the woods.

Several days passed and Rusty moped. However as he lay at Carl's feet one evening there was a familiar scratching on the door and the knob began to turn. Rusty and Carl went to see what visitor had come this evening.

When Snoopy ambled into the room, he touched noses with Rusty, whose tail was wagging his whole body. Immediately the two started wrestling more vigorously than ever before. When they finished their romp they were panting and exhausted, but obviously wonderfully contented. Soon they went over to Rusty's corner where they curled up together for a long night's sleep.

The beloved Rusty, who had come like a copper streak to greet every guest, human or animal, died quietly at last and went to what Carl calls "the Cathedral of the Pines," there to meet his old friends Louie, Snoopy and so many others. A big stone and bronze memorial marker was erected above his grave, and in enduring letters the epitaph reads:

NORTHERNAIRE'S
beloved
"RUSTY"
Friend and Protector
of
Woodland Orphans and Man
He Taught us an Unforgettable Lesson
in
Tolerance, Patience and Loyalty

Ginger with a fawn, one hour after they met

Seven or eight months before Rusty died, his beautiful daughter Ginger was born. This gave Carl the chance to test his theory that a dog can be taught to love and protect wild animals. Rusty had needed no training in this respect, being diplomatic, friendly and wise by instinct. Now in his old age he began to teach his puppy how to play with, and care for, baby otters, raccoons, badgers, foxes, little bears, skunks and even porcupines. Carl also helped in the training, warning Ginger to approach any new animal very slowly.

"Slow, girl! Take it easy," Carl would say.

Soon the little cocker was almost as proficient as her father in sensing the mood of each new foundling. Usually within a matter of minutes, and always within an hour or two, Ginger was able to gain the confidence of these woodland playmates. When Rusty died, Carl had but one consolation: Ginger had willingly taken over the responsibilities inherited from her father.

There was a noticeable difference between the two spaniels, however. Rusty had been laughing and playful, utterly joyous in his relationship to all the animals. Perhaps Ginger was burdened too young. She was endlessly tolerant, letting Ouch the porcupine lick her ear for many minutes at a time, and allowing the otters and little foxes to climb all over her. But she did not laugh quite as often as her father had and was a little less playful. Frequently she had an expression of worried concern on her face. As in the case of her father, she represented deputized authority over all the animals. And her rule was seldom questioned even by the bears who were often ten times her size.

Only once did Bopper test Ginger's courage. He could boast many times the weight of the little dog and seemed certain that he could intimidate her. Perhaps he was a trifle jealous of Carl's affection for the spaniel. Bopper approached slowly, slapped his tail loudly on the floor and hissed. Ginger stood her ground proudly, while the other animals watched with fascination. Bopper lunged toward the dog, but did not actually attack. Ginger growled a stern warning. Realizing he had failed in his bluff, Bopper lay on his side and played dead like an opossum. From that moment forward, all of the animals seemed to realize that

Ginger with two fox kits and a baby otter

Ginger "spoke for" Carl Marty and deserved their respect and obedience.

While Ginger was still young, she was faced with a problem which might have been far more formidable than Bopper's bluff. A woman living in Rhinelander, Wisconsin called Carl Marty to ask if he would be willing to adopt a full-grown, fifty-pound brush wolf named Lulu. She assured Carl that Lulu was tame and affectionate, but said that hunters had nearly beaten the poor animal to death with their gun butts almost at her front door. She now had to keep her chained in the back yard or locked in the house for her own protection.

Carl Marty seldom refuses to care for any endangered animal, and he had his own theories about wolves. Like all of us who have studied the history of the dog, he knew that the very first animals domesticated by the cavemen were wolf puppies, left motherless when the parents were slain. He also knew that almost all breeds of modern dogs have descended from these wild ancestors. Can the wolf be so dangerous?

In Canada, standing awards have been offered for authentic proof of any wolf attacking a man. No claimant has come forward. Wolves do indeed follow woodsmen out of curiosity, but at a safe distance, sometimes finding food scraps near dead campfires as the men move on.

Only one remaining doubt made Carl hesitate. Could Ginger, little more than a puppy, discipline a full-grown wolf? He looked down at the small, serious dog lying at his feet and felt a new confidence remembering the remarkable way in which Ginger handled the bears.

"I'll be glad to take Lulu on one condition," Carl said. "I won't cage her or chain her. She must have her freedom to go and come as she likes."

Carl admits that he was a bit fearful not only for Ginger but for all the other pets when the lady drove in with Lulu. The wolf took one look at the spaniel, and both approached slowly, with tails wagging. Wolf and dog touched noses. Lulu leaped in the air and so did Ginger. Then they began to play and to chase each other all over the lawn and through the woods. There would be no need for Ginger to fear this new friend who romped with her as might another dog, and sometimes slept with her at night.

"Lulu was one of the gentlest pets we have ever had," Carl said. "She played with the otters, raccoons and all the other animals, and was particularly tender with the fawns. Most of the guests at Northernaire thought she was a big dog. But many of the neighbors and some of the hunters knew she was a wolf.

"The myths about the ferocity of wolves prejudice children at an early age. Even such seemingly harmless stories as 'Little Red Riding Hood' misinform them and terrify them with the canard that any wolf might eat your grandmother. The rumor spread that Lulu was leading a whole pack of wolves. And although I took her to visit the game warden to prove her gentleness, neighbors continued to complain that I was harboring a killer.

"Several hunters took shots at Lulu, and finally one wounded her so badly that she could not live. She came in bleeding and imploring us to be helpful, but there was nothing we could do. And so passed one of the most affectionate and harmless of all our animals."

Lulu was not the only victim of ignorance, prejudice and sheer sadism. Pet deer clearly marked with red ribbons and with antlers stained with Mercurochrome are murdered almost every year by poachers, usually as the trusting animal walks to within ten or fifteen feet of these "licensed murderers" invading posted land. A tame red fox named Ragmop had his head bashed in by another great "sportsman," and a doe which had given Carl Marty several pairs of twin fawns—a pet so tame it ate from the hand of any guest—was found in the nearby woods one hunting season with its throat cut with a knife.

"It is fortunate we never caught that man," said the usually gentle Carl, "or is it? There is a law much higher than the game laws. It is the law of decency, and of love for the animals who for thousands of years roamed and 'owned' these forests before man came to despoil them. Such slaughterers of gentle pets are doomed to live with their consciences, if indeed a man like that has a conscience."

Carl Marty's love of all the animals of his region definitely extends to the bears. The common black bear *(Euarctos americanus)* is native to all but four states. They have a cinnamon phase in the West and a blue phase in Alaska. But whatever their tint, these ursine panhandlers are potentially dangerous if only because of their size and their swiftness.

Black bears are not as heavy nor as rapid as grizzlies which sometimes attain a weight of one thousand five hundred pounds, or more, and can travel at a top speed of thirty-five miles an hour. Nevertheless the grizzly's little cousin can also be formidable. He sometimes weighs six or seven hundred pounds at maturity, and can run and climb much faster than a trained athlete. Carl thinks there is no truth in stories told by hunters who claim to have outrun a bear and then "climbed to safety in a tree."

I must admit that I do not trust bears as much as Carl Marty does. But I also admit that my contacts have been fewer. Carl has never been injured by any of the seven bears he has protected at Northernaire; but most of them came to him as babies and were reared with tenderness and affection. Like Joy Adamson's lioness, Elsa, these bear cubs grew up as part of the family and were, in effect, his children. But even Carl does not advise teasing a bear, or coming between a mother bear and her cubs. He was greatly concerned when Irene Castle, one of his frequent guests, impulsively insisted upon "wrestling" with a full-grown bear they met in the woods. Fortunately she came off unscathed, although the outcome might have been tragically different.

Once when I was photographing bears in the Great Smoky Mountains National Park near Gatlinburg, Tennessee, I attempted a close-up that proved to be too close for comfort. Adjusting the portrait lens on my Zeiss Ikon to focus at a distance of six feet, I opened the door of the automobile and stepped to the ground. The big black bear, who apparently thought I was offering her food, made a good-natured pass at the camera, which I pulled out of her reach as I hastily stepped back into the car, slamming the door behind me. A split second later her well-armed front paw hit the glass with a blow that shook the car. Her aim was perfect. That was where my face had been a moment before. Luckily the glass did not break, but I had learned my lesson.

Carl, however, has an uncanny understanding of bears. He is an excellent animal psychologist and can always anticipate the exact mood of these big clowns. Furthermore he has found the bears of northern Wisconsin to be universally harmless in the wilds. It is only the *tame* wild bear which may be potentially dangerous. The way Carl raises bears, however, demonstrates what good care and affection can do to develop the fundamental gentleness which lies just beneath their shaggy exterior.

"Our first bear, Annie, was still a cub when the game warden brought her," Carl told me. "In contrast to aggressive ferocity, the first time she saw a fawn she was so frightened that she scrambled up a tree. The bear weighed thirty-five pounds, and the baby fawn one-fifth as much. It took a week for the bear to begin to trust the gentle and inquisitive fawn.

"Annie enjoyed people from the moment she arrived. Various friends of the little bear would take her for walks in the woods,

but on the way back to the hotel, Annie would become tired; and when she got tired, she got tired all over. She would then stage a sit-down strike until someone picked her up and carried her home like a baby, with her paws around his neck.

"One day Annie walked into the lounge and bar. She saw other people sitting on stools so she decided to do the same. The bartender had an inspiration. He took a cold bottle of grape pop, and using an ice pick, punched a hole in the metal cap. This looked so much like her nursing bottle that Annie picked it up and began to suck lustily. From that day until she was full grown, Annie was our best grape-pop customer.

"Many times a guest coming in from the bright sunshine to the comparatively dim light of the lounge did a double-take when he saw a bear sitting on the stool beside him. Sometimes women would scream and make a hasty departure.

"One day Annie wandered upstairs and walked into the open door of a room occupied by a single lady, who thereupon uttered a blood-curdling yell. Annie was terrified and bounded down the stairs. She was trembling and asking for protection as I walked in. When I reached the lobby, the woman was there relating her story. Fortunately she was laughing about the experience. Much as we loved Annie, we decided that a public hotel is no place for a full-grown bear."

Carl Marty continued to have interesting experiences with bears, who as cubs are among the most charming and playful pets one could wish. The baby bears brought to him were seldom less than three months old, since their first weeks are spent in the den where the mother is enjoying her drowsy winter. It is true that

OPPOSITE / *Little bear at Northernaire*

bears do not really hibernate in the sense that the woodchuck does. Their temperature does not drop precipitously nor their heartbeat slow to a point that seems near death. But the sleep is so deep that a female bear is not always aware when her cubs are born. These little creatures (one, two or three in number) usually weigh considerably less than a pound. While their mother continues to sleep, they nurse with contentment, huddle next to her for warmth, and soon begin to climb all over her massive body and explore the dim cave in which they live. At about six weeks the mother may awake sufficiently to take her first look at her cubs whose bright eyes are now wide open. By this time they wrestle playfully, have fine coats of soft fur and weigh about two pounds.

Usually the mother takes another nap before the spring sun melts the snowdrifts over the den. The new warmth makes the cubs so lively that further sleep becomes impossible. The big bear looks from the mouth of the little cave and sees a few tufts of green grass and the earliest flowers. She yawns, stretches and leads the impatient cubs into the sunlit world, where in the coming weeks she teaches them to catch fish, eat grass, dig roots, tear open bee trees to get honey and to obey her when she growls a stern warning. The little bears, who up to this time have had no discipline, resist any restraint upon their mischief. It takes many slaps, nips and growls to make them become good little bears.

If tragedy overtakes their protective mother, however, the cubs are forlorn. One such mother with triplets put her foot in a wolf trap, and next morning was shot by the trapper. The three pitiful cubs followed their dead mother as she was dragged from the woods. They were captured and brought to Carl Marty, who never turns away an orphan creature. Placed in a box in his bedroom, and covered with blankets, they soon made their way into his warm bed, having substituted him for their natural protector.

Later they went back to the woods to live their own lives, but would sometimes come to the animal house, which was now called "Ginger's House" in honor of the hostess.

Little bears are one thing, but big bears are another, as Carl Marty discovered when he tangled with Tanga. Carl has always maintained that if he raised a bear cub in the woods, they could share a cabin—even sleep together—and neither would have to worry about being harmed. He had a chance to test his theory, not

Bear meets fawn

with a cub he had reared, but with a nearly mature bear named Tanga whom he met at seven one evening and went to bed with at nine.

The people who had raised her from babyhood were moving south. They had asked Carl to adopt their "tame bear" and Carl had agreed, with the same stipulation he had made concerning the wolf. The bear must be allowed to have her complete freedom.

However, when Tanga arrived, she was wearing a collar and a short, stout chain. The ex-owners explained that they always chained Tanga to a ring in the floor each night because she was sometimes mischievous. This was against Carl's principles, but on this busy evening he had no time to make friends with the bear, so he asked one of his staff to attach a ring to the floor of his bedroom in a nearby cabin.

When Tanga's chain was snapped to the ring, she started complaining, gave Carl a suspicious look, and decided to test the strength of the fastening. The floor boards began to bulge.

Obviously this was not the solution, so Carl unsnapped the chain. The bear, in a switch on the Goldilocks story, began to explore the kitchen, the living room and the rest of the little house. A ladder to the open-deck attic offered additional adventure, and Tanga climbed up to see what she could find. She threw down deer antlers, Christmas tree decorations and extra blankets. Finally Carl was able to coax her down with the offer of a tempting meal.

It was obvious that Tanga was mischievous, but Carl was not yet convinced that she was dangerous. His whole philosophy rebelled at the thought that she might do him harm if they spent the night together. At the moment she seemed peaceful enough, stretched out at the foot of his bed.

"I sat down on the bed beside her and gently stroked her black fur," Carl relates. "Then I bared my forearm and extended it toward her, hoping she would respond in the manner of other bears—and she did. She took the skin of my forearm between her lips and began to purr like an outboard motor.

"Here was my chance to demonstrate to myself that I could sleep with a big bear. I got into my pajamas and slid between the covers, careful not to startle my bed partner who was still stretched across the foot of the bed. For lack of space I had to pull my knees nearly up to my chin—a rather uncomfortable position for sleeping."

Apparently Carl is not afflicted with nightmares nor insomnia. Perhaps a clear conscience helps, as does the fresh, pine-laden air of the North Woods. He fell pleasantly asleep and did not awaken until he felt a friendly arm on his shoulder. Carl was now in a normal sleeping position, and in the moonlight he could see a black, furry head on the pillow beside him.

"It occurred to me that I was exposing myself unnecessarily to some possible scratches," Carl said. "So I rolled over on my stomach, and put my face in the crook of my arm. Now if the bear had bad dreams, the most I would lose would be an ear. In this position I again fell into a sound and dreamless sleep.

"The next time I awoke was at four-fifteen. I was aware of an almost suffocating weight upon me. Not only was the bear lying athwart my body, but she had somehow embraced me with both powerful forearms. I could feel the big claws of both front paws on my cheekbones. I had never before felt the slightest fear of bears. But I will admit that I was now somewhat concerned. I could feel my heart beating faster than usual, and I was very uncomfortable. But I decided that this was no time to panic. So I lay absolutely motionless."

Eventually almost any bed partner rolls over, and Tanga was no exception. Soon her head was again on her own pillow, and that front paw was resting rather easily on Carl's shoulder. Carl had proved his point. He could sleep with a large, unknown bear. Now he was free to retrieve one of the extra blankets Tanga had thrown down from the attic, and to curl up on the davenport for what remained of the night.

Carl Marty was so relieved to have even the davenport to himself that he slept until after sunrise. He was awakened this time by a very odd noise in the kitchen. Tanga liked her breakfast early and was feeling frustrated. To show her displeasure, she was busy ripping the linoleum from the kitchen floor. Carl realized she was hungry. He quickly arose to feed his guest a large breakfast. After that he opened the back door and told the bear she could return for another meal whenever she liked. But he hoped that from then on she would be content to live in the woods.

For the next several days nothing was seen or heard of Tanga. It was a pleasant autumn, with the usual wild burst of color in the foliage, and the annual harvest of the forest spread bountifully beneath the trees. Carl imagined that Tanga had found a big hollow log or small cave in which to live, and that she would be so intrigued with her new freedom that she would make her visits to Northernaire fairly infrequent.

Late one afternoon, however, he had a call from a member of the staff. A frantic voice informed him that Tanga was on top of the recreation building, tearing off the shingles.

"I left word not to disturb her," Carl recalls. "After all, one can always replace shingles or linoleum, but it is not every day that a playful bear perches on your roof.

"I hurried to the building to find Tanga straddling the peak. As I stood watching, she deliberately peeled off a shingle. It came loose with a satisfying rip and she sent it sailing through the air. She looked down at me coyly and then tore off another shingle. As though she were plucking petals from a daisy, she stripped off one shingle after another."

Carl would have preferred to remain watching these antics, but dusk had fallen and he was needed to take his accustomed place at the door of the Showboat nearby, where he greeted his evening guests arriving for music, entertainment and dancing.

Tanga watched Carl enter that intriguing building, and saw about two hundred other people from the hotel gaily passing through the same door. Then she heard music and laughter and seemed to realize that she was missing an evening which might furnish even more fun than pulling shingles from a roof.

"It wasn't long," Carl said, "before I saw Tanga pacing back and forth in front of the Showboat. She apparently had made up her mind that she wanted to see the performance. When she walked in, she had the poise of visiting royalty.

"We have an unwritten law which gives any animal star billing. No matter who may be on stage, the spotlight is turned on the four-footed visitor. We had often welcomed deer, ranging from small fawns to eight-point bucks, but we had never before entertained such a big bear. She skirted the bar and headed for the theater lounge.

"I stepped to the microphone and broke into the show with the announcement that we were about to see something quite unusual. I asked the audience to make no noise or movement that might startle our special guest—even if they themselves were startled.

"The orchestra picked up my cue to continue, and our vocalist, Rose Marie Bell, found herself unexpectedly sharing the stage with a partner she had never met before. With Tanga at her side, she managed with amazing bravado to smile and sing her number as though this were an everyday occurrence.

"At the end of the song, Tanga stepped down from the stage and took a leisurely tour of the circle of tables around it. Some of the guests were thrilled, some amused, and a few may have been frightened, but they didn't show it.

"Tanga apparently was already bored by a night-club life. Having proved that she could behave beautifully when out in company, she wandered through the bar and out the door. I do not know where she spent that winter. We saw her once in a while at the edge of the woods, a contented bear, who in all probability would eventually have cubs while she slept in some warm den far beneath the snowdrifts."

Henry David Thoreau, one of America's first conservationists, realized the sad truth concerning the average outdoorsman. "How base are the motives which commonly carry men into the wilderness. They have no more love for wild nature than woodsawyers have for forests. For one that comes to sketch, or to sing, a thousand come with axe or rifle."

Carl Marty, who loves nature as did Thoreau, has always been dismayed by the senseless slaughter when thousands of deer hunters descend upon northern Wisconsin on the opening day of the season, killing almost anything that comes within rifle range, including occasional cows and horses. These gunmen who had murdered so many of his pets have scant knowledge concerning the animals they shoot.

But there are other outdoorsmen who never carry a gun, and this better breed has increased since Thoreau's day. Hearing by grapevine of Carl Marty and his animals, these creative people began coming to Northernaire. Among them were several famous photographers such as Wallace Kirkland, Art Wittman and Grant Halliday (who managed to find and photograph in these woods sixteen native varieties of wild orchids). Distinguished writers including August Derleth and Leo Lerner helped Carl to reach an ever widening circle with the good news that forest creatures are safe in at least one protected part of northern Wisconsin. Carl founded the Three Lakes Wilderness Society, to which he donated much time and all the income from his own writing. He thus managed to increase by thousands of acres the area where animals can live their natural lives free of the fear of man. Conservation societies began to make the hotel the site of their annual conventions. Here they could meet Ginger's friends in person, and see the movies Carl had made of his peaceable kingdom where "the lion and the lamb" (or at least the bear and the fawn) lie down together. When Ginger watched the film she often rushed to the silver screen to touch noses with the otters, raccoons, deer, badgers, skunks, porcupines, foxes and other creatures who had come so often to have a meal and a romp in her well-furnished little house.

After ten eventful years, Ginger died peacefully in 1958. But she had already helped to teach Bernese, a huge young St. Bernard, to take her place. And although Bernese has proved to be great-hearted and tender, guarding all the animals, Ginger still haunts Carl's memory. At dusk he can almost see the golden spaniel moving among her guests at the hostelry for forest animals which will always be maintained in memory of Ginger.

Animal generations come and go with a swift rhythm. Most of the wild creatures of Ginger's era did not outlast her. Ouch and Ooh, the friendly porcupines; Henrietta, the female raccoon who returned each season with a new litter of kits; Bopper, the beaver; Lulu, the wolf, and many of the badgers and foxes had long since gone to their happy hunting ground.

But at least one beloved animal, Sugar, the otter, outlived Ginger by five years and became a fast friend of Bernese, the St. Bernard. Carl obtained the twin otter babies, Sugar and Spice, in 1950. Spice was caught by a trapper during the open season of the following spring under a vicious Wisconsin law which allows extensive trapping of this increasingly rare species.

Up the raccoon hatch to visit Ginger

For nearly thirteen years Sugar remained Carl's closest animal companion, sometimes sleeping with him, swimming beside him in the lake and following him along the shore. No more faithful or dependable pet has ever lived at Northernaire. Free to go wherever she liked on that long chain of lakes, Sugar was seldom beyond call. Carl has spent months of his time and thousands of dollars to protect the maligned and persecuted otter, and his unassailable arguments in their defense will be summarized in the final chapter of this book. No one who has known these play-ful, inquisitive, highly intelligent animals can forgive the state "conservationists" who have virtually doomed them to eventual extinction in Wisconsin.

Fortunately Carl Marty, and his three gentle dogs, have never been the only shepherds of the wild flock at Northernaire. Various members of the staff have become emotionally involved. Among Carl's most enthusiastic and devoted pupils is Leslie Carroll, a

But Ginger has gone on a long journey, so Carl plays host

Leslie Carroll and a raccoon visit a fawn

talented dancer and animal trainer. She is the daughter of aerial
artists, long featured by the Ringling Circus, and she lives with
her mother in a cabin in the woods where she spends more time
rearing orphan animals than she does under the spotlight at the
Showboat. The dogs in her act were unfortunate waifs, doomed
to extermination by a pound-keeper. They were trained entirely
without punishment and solely with affection.

Calamity Jack is called from the woods to get his bottle

He kisses his good friend Bernese, who has been his seeing-eye dog

And now for that comforting bottle of warm milk (with vitamins added)

When Carl Marty has given a fox, raccoon or otter several days of his personal care, he turns the little animal over to Leslie for the next few weeks. Carl's only complaint is that Miss Carroll continues to protect each animal longer than is necessary.

It is a scene from a fairy story, or from one of the better Disney animations, to see fawns, fox kits and little raccoons following Leslie's footsteps along the woodland paths.

During the summer of 1965, Carl, Leslie and the St. Bernard faced a formidable task. A tiny spotted fawn was brought to Northernaire totally blind and suffering from a hernia. A good animal surgeon operated and cured the hernia, but warned that the blindness might be incurable. Carl fed the small creature with warm milk to which he added greatly fortified doses of the proper vitamins, and slowly a miraculous change occurred. Little by little the fawn began to regain its sight. Bernese became his inseparable companion—probably the only two-hundred-pound, seeing-eye dog that a seven-pound fawn has ever had. The diminutive buck began to run and leap like other small deer, but in an unfortunate fall, broke a fragile front leg. Placed in a cast, Calamity Jack was not long subdued, but continued to race through the dim world of shadowy trees.

"When one has had full vision and loses half of it, that is a tragedy," Carl said. "But when one has been totally blind and regains fifty percent of his vision, that is a miracle—a rebirth from darkness into the realm of light." Now when Carl calls, Jack races out of the forest, the gayest, most affectionate fawn ever seen at Northernaire.

SIX

Long Live the Wilderness

When the French and the English began to settle the North American continent, the abundance of wild life throughout the unexplored wilderness was almost unimaginable. Wild ducks and geese rose in clouds from the bays and estuaries. Wild turkeys and white-tailed deer were so numerous and unafraid of man that any hunter could easily supply his family with food by walking half a mile through the forest. Passenger pigeons frequently darkened the sky from horizon to horizon. They constituted nearly one third of the total bird life, and the continental flock at the beginning of the nineteenth century has been estimated at five billion. Bison ranged from the Pacific to a scattering on the Atlantic. Estimates of their numbers on the western plains range from ten million to one hundred million.

In the days before mill dams and pollution discouraged and

finally obliterated most of the eastern salmon runs, that delicious game fish was almost as abundant in some of the New England rivers as on the Pacific Coast. Every clear stream of cool water was alive with trout, and in the deeper lakes and rivers lived myriads of other fish, ranging in size up to the mighty sturgeon, which sometimes weighed hundreds of pounds.

Despite the Indians with their flint-tipped arrows, there was no danger to any species, for the Indian lived in harmony with the land. The animals and the birds of the forest were his brothers, and although he killed what he needed for food and clothing, he often asked forgiveness of their spirits, now free to live eternally along the flowering meadows of the Milky Way. It would have been impossible for the Indian or the early white settler to imagine that within three centuries every passenger pigeon would be slaughtered, all but a pitiful remnant of the vast buffalo herds would be obliterated by "sportsmen" (who killed as many as a million a year taking only the tongues and the hides). Our ancestors could not know that heedless and wanton hunters would all but exterminate the whooping crane, the trumpeter swan and the bald eagle.

The biological Eden of North America had no counterpart in the entire world. Here was a continent so rich and fertile that its natural resources seemed inexhaustible. A verdant canopy of ever-greens and broad-leafed trees stretched from coast to coast (except where prairies and plains nourished the buffalo, and snow-capped peaks harbored the bighorn sheep and the mountain goat). The mainly equable climate was perfect for man and beast. East of the 100th meridian and again in a wide band along the Pacific Coast, there was sufficient rainfall to grow any crop of the temperate zone. Even the more arid regions, with their scenic grandeur, supported plants and animals native to the area.

Europe was crowded, and in many parts overtilled and overgrazed. Sheep and the plow had already destroyed the sylvan glades and crystal fountains of classic Greece and Rome. Spain too was mostly barren and eroded. But North America had miraculously escaped the "blessings" of civilization. Here, if anywhere in the world, there was a chance for a new start, if only man had the intelligence and the integrity to work *with* nature instead of *against* her. The "ecology" of this pristine continent was the last, best hope of mankind. Here every form of life from the microbe to the moose, from the meadow mouse to the grizzly bear, and from the hummingbird to the eagle composed an interrelated and interdependent balance of nature that was like a great symphony orchestra.

But our "rude forefathers," who had so many other rugged virtues, had no slightest inkling of the harmony they were disrupting. They were too busy cutting and burning the trees, fighting the "savages" and killing game, to do much serious thinking.

The more ambitious saw the golden opportunity of making a quick fortune by stripping New England, New York and the Great Lakes states of all their valuable lumber, and finally looting the mineral wealth of the *West*. It meant nothing to them that a California redwood tree might have been growing to its majestic proportions for two or three thousand years. They estimated its value in board feet. Burning the brush behind them, they started forest fires that *in a single year* destroyed twenty-five million acres of virgin forest, an area approximately the size of all the national parks at the present time.

Most of the damage to our continent was done during the nineteenth century when land was cheap, political morals lax, and the general public abysmally ignorant of the fact that our major wealth was being stolen by the robber barons and the "Empire Builders." Only gradually did we awake from the pleasant dream of inexhaustible resources.

One of the first voices crying in the wilderness and warning us of impending doom was Henry David Thoreau. The area around Concord (where he spent his entire life, except for his brief trips to Cape Cod, Maine and Canada) was already showing signs of land mismanagement. There were a few abandoned farms, one of which he briefly thought of buying. None of the larger wild animals lived in the vicinity of his hut on Walden pond. Deer, moose, bear and cougar had long since been exterminated. Erosion was beginning to take the topsoil from upland pastures and orchards. Thoreau longed for "wilder wildness." He saw that "the mass of men live lives of quiet desperation," and he thought that one way to free them was to lure them outdoors. For this purpose there would need to be parks and recreation areas.

Thoreau was one of our first true conservationists. "Each town should have a park," he wrote, "or rather a primitive forest of five hundred or a thousand acres . . . a common possession forever."

Many years before our national government set aside Yosemite or Yellowstone, Thoreau was asking, "Why should not we have our national preserves? . . . not for idle sport or food, but for inspiration and our own true recreation."

The next such poet of nature to really stir the general imagination was Thoreau's Pacific Coast counterpart, John Muir, for whom a lake, a sequoia grove, a glacier, a mountain peak and a butterfly have been named. Muir was born in Scotland, spent most of his boyhood on a farm in Wisconsin and reached California in March 1868, where a new and glorious life opened to this ever-perceptive lover of wilderness beauty.

He tramped alone through the "Range of Light," as he always called the Sierras, and fell in love with Yosemite, fighting for four decades to save this valley for the nation and for "generations yet unborn." Not until he enlisted the powerful help of Theodore Roosevelt during a memorable night beside their campfire could

*HE MAKETH ME TO LIE DOWN IN GREEN PASTURES;
HE LEADETH ME BESIDE THE STILL WATERS*

he be relatively certain that his lifelong struggle to protect his beloved wilderness area would be successful.

Muir was the sort of man for whom wilderness is a religion. Once in a great windstorm, when nature was holding "high festi-

val," he climbed to the topmost branches of a tall pine and stayed there through the wildest part of the gale, swaying twenty or thirty degrees at each gust while forest giants fell around him. He gloried in the music, giving little thought to his danger.

There were other heroes in this long battle to preserve and conserve the greatest of our natural treasures, the life-sustaining, life-giving wilderness. Carl Schurz, Gifford Pinchot, Stephen Mather, both Roosevelts, John F. Kennedy and Lyndon B. Johnson and his wife have all contributed in varying degrees. John D. Rockefeller, Jr., not only donated tens of millions of dollars, but much time, energy and careful planning to the great cause. The Audubon Society and hundreds of other organizations have helped to fight off the ruthless despoilers of our continent.

Through education, a large part of our population has become conservation-minded. But there are still millions of utterly selfish individuals who kill, pillage, litter and pollute. Tragically enough, much of this destruction of our priceless heritage is encouraged, or at least permitted by government agencies.

In the public mind there is much confusion concerning the relationship of the National Parks to the National Forests. Actually there are many basic differences. The parks are admirably administered to "preserve for all time" the wonders within their boundaries. They completely protect wild life from hunters and trappers, the forests from the lumber interests, and the plant life from cattle and sheep growers. Oil men and miners are not allowed to extract the mineral wealth, and the building of private cabins and business structures is prohibited. The National Park Service is part of the Department of the Interior and is subject to far less political pressure than that which burdens the Forest Service which is operated by the Department of Agriculture.

In 1905 Theodore Roosevelt and Gifford Pinchot pushed through the bill which transferred federal forest land from Interior to Agriculture. Up to this time Pinchot and Muir had been friends and fellow conservationists. Now they were scarcely on a speaking basis. For Muir saw far more clearly than Pinchot that the National Forest Act opened an area many times that of the National Parks to exploitation and abuses. "Controlled" lumbering, mining and hunting are allowed in the National Forests. Sheep and cattle are allowed to graze. A very disturbing book could be written concerning the damage this policy has done to our dwindling wilderness.

We are still passing conservation acts which help to defeat their own purpose. For instance Public Law 88-577, popularly known as the Wilderness Act, was widely hailed when it was passed in September 1964. But I wonder how many citizens read the act or understood the true meaning of the single sentence of small type which says: (8) *Nothing in this Act shall be construed as affecting the jurisdiction or responsibilities of the several States with respect to wildlife and fish in the national forests.*

In plain English, state game laws apply to most of these federal wilderness areas. The state conservation departments, which usually subsist on fees paid for hunting and fishing licenses, have a strong tendency to virtually capitulate to the powerful political groups armed with sporting rifles and shotguns. There are, of course, a few well-trained biologists and botanists and true conservationists scattered through these departments in the more progressive states. I agree with Carl Marty that we could scarcely achieve even a minimum of protection for animals without the help of some of these farsighted and humane men. But they are usually in a minority. Some of our backward states appear to be brutally unconcerned about even the most rare and endangered species. Any edible bird or animal is nothing but "game" to them. They speak of "harvesting" even the gentle dove and cheerful bobwhite. Most of the pamphlets they distribute show an incredible ignorance of the animals and birds they are supposed to "protect."

As a single instance of the type of "conservation" being practiced all over the United States, we might take the river otter, which may eventually follow the sea otter, which also faces possible extinction.

The otter, like the raccoon, is an extremely intelligent, playful, clean and affectionate animal. At one time there were thought to be fifty thousand in Wisconsin alone. At this time the trout fishing was legendary. Today the Wisconsin otter has almost vanished and trout fishing is poor.

The point is that the otter, contrary to almost universal superstition, eats almost no trout, but does eat enormous numbers of crayfish which eat trout eggs and spawn. One of the best ways to increase the trout population in a stream is to introduce a few otters. Carl Marty, watching the alarming depletion of otters in northern Wisconsin, called a conference of several of the leading otter experts of America including Emil Liers, who has raised scores of otters and written several books about them. The men made a tape recording of their conversation which contains some very convincing testimony.

"I had the mistaken notion that otters fed on fish," said Liers, speaking of his early experiences, "so I fed them fish, and lo and behold! I found that a steady fish diet caused a kind of anemia and then paralysis. Every pound of raw fish you feed an otter uses three thousand units of vitamin B_1, taking it out of the system."

What few fish the otter does eat are slower, coarser varieties. He is not swift enough to catch a trout unless it is sick or stranded in a shallow pool. Examination of fifty stomachs of otters at the University of Minnesota showed only minute traces of trout, but quantities of crayfish.

Most shocking of all, the open season on otters in Wisconsin is during the whelping period from late February to early April. This means that for every nursing mother caught in a trap, two baby otters are left to starve to death.

The now-famous otter tape was sent to the Wisconsin Conservation Commission which for once made a humane decision. It closed the entire state to otter trapping for one year. But the trout fishermen (whom I prefer to consider "sportsmen" since I raise and fish trout myself) put so much pressure on the state government that it completely reversed itself, and for the last ten years has allowed the all-but-extinct otter to again be trapped during whelping season. Fortunately Carl Marty's personal efforts have induced private land owners around him to close twenty-five thousand acres to all trapping and hunting, and in the autumn of 1965 Carl was again finding a few signs of the otter on his chain of lakes.

A remarkably similar plea can be made for the raccoon, which eats millions of crayfish, snakes, turtles and insects but is far too slow to catch a trout. The species is not now as endangered as it was in the 1920's when the price of raccoon pelts rose to an all-time high in the effort to satisfy the silly whims of flappers and sheiks on college campuses. Several famous raccoon states had to close or limit the season to keep the raccoon from becoming only a memory. But before raccoons had made a real comeback, seasons were opened again.

After Pearl Harbor most men of the raccoon-hunting age went off to join a grimmer hunt in the Pacific and in Europe. But the salvation of the raccoon, in this writer's estimation, was the disappearance of the raccoon-coat fad, the precipitous drop in pelt prices, and the development of synthetic fibers which produce coats that look like fur and do not bulk out the figure to Burl Ives proportions.

Thus the rescue of the raccoon, like the rescue of the beaver, was not a moral regeneration but an economic factor. Beaver hats went out of style in the late 1830's, pelt prices plummeted, and the beaver was saved. Otherwise John Jacob Astor might have added a few more million dollars to his hoard, and the overdramatized "Mountain Men" might have exterminated the last family of beavers on the continent.

The raccoon has survived for another reason, however. He is perhaps the most intelligent, and certainly the most dexterous and adaptable mammal in North America, barring only man himself. He can sleep almost anywhere, eat almost anything, master almost any lock, zipper or can lid. After thousands of hours watching, feeding and playing with raccoons, I believe as I did as a boy that they are actively evolving toward a higher form.

As Thoreau suggested, all living things are better off alive than dead, be they man, moose or pine tree. And as John Muir believed, man cannot even survive without the wilderness to freshen his mind and revive his perception. We are but the ephemera of the moment, the brief custodians of redwoods, which were ancient when Christ was born, and of the birds of the air and animals of the forest which have been evolving for countless millenniums. We do not own the land we abuse, or the lakes and streams we pollute or the raccoons and the otters which we persecute. Those who play God in destroying any form of life are tampering with a master plan too intricate for any of us to understand. All that we can do is to aid that great plan and to keep part of our planet habitable. The greatest predator on earth is man himself, and we must look inward to destroy the killer instinct which may yet atomize the human race. Our morality must be extended to every living thing upon our globe, and we must amend the Golden Rule to read: "Do unto all other creatures as you would have them do unto you!"

With Gratitude

People who love and protect animals have other generous impulses. I am indebted to scores of intelligent naturalists, conservationists, photographers, neighbors and friends for sharing their experiences and thus enriching this book.

Carl Marty of Northernaire placed at my disposal many of his nature notes and tapes, plus a sheaf of photographs which could not be duplicated. Equally helpful was Leonard Lee Rue III, a friend and fellow naturalist, who has spent a creative lifetime photographing the flora and fauna of New Jersey.

Probably the best way to acknowledge my thanks to those who have contributed materially to this book is to trace the sources, and identify the pictures, a chapter at a time.

CHAPTER ONE

The text of the first chapter is based almost entirely upon my memory and that of my wife, Gladys. Alone, we might be fallible. But we have never been alone. The photograph on the jacket (which is also the frontispiece) was taken by my son-in-law Clarence E. Olson, an editor on the St. Louis *Post-Dispatch*. The pictures of Gladys, and of her hands packaging egges, are from the camera of Reed I. MacDonald, husband of my sister Jessica. I made the portraits of my son David and my daughter Arielle. Most of the other pictures in Chapter One were taken by Leonard Rue.

CHAPTER TWO

The text of the second chapter is again based upon mutual memories, plus a diary which I began to keep at about this time. All of the pictures are by Leonard Rue except the last one of the emerging raccoon kits which was focused through the perceptive lens of F. W. Stuewer, who wrote his brilliant doctoral thesis on raccoons.

CHAPTER THREE

Letters from Harriett E. Weaver, Harry James, Nora Evans and Sylvia Summerland assisted me in formulating the text of the third chapter. Don Meadows took the picture of Miss Weaver. Harry James clicked the shutter on the raccoons embellishing his anecdotes. Jessie Smith, a prize-winning photographer, captured the portraits of Nora Evans' bright bell-ringers. Glenn Zahn of Cleveland immortalized George Schuster's carroon bread-line, and Leonard Rue snapped Mischa watching television.

CHAPTER FOUR

Various articulate friends and correspondents increased my knowledge concerning raccoons as pets. I am particularly grateful to Mrs. Buc, Jane and Norman Schultz, Gordon Blandford, Ted and Olivia Smith, Wayne Adkins and his family and Bob and Hazel Jones for authenticated stories about their raccoons. The pictures in this chapter are by four talented photographers. Leonard Rue owned the baby raccoon drinking from the bottle. Ed Bry surprised the ring-tailed rascal milking the family cow. Clarence Olson took all the pictures of me with the twin raccoons and the pictures of this same pair turning on the hose and skirting the baptismal pool. Finally it was the talented W. J. Collings, Jr., of the Weyerhaeuser Company who photographed the remarkable gallery featuring Tinker and the Adkins family.

CHAPTER FIVE

Carl Marty helped me assemble all the photographs taken at his resort Northernaire at Three Lakes, Wisconsin, and has given me the permission to use them. Where the photographers can be remembered or identified, they are Arthur Witman who took the second, third, fourth and eleventh pictures in this chapter; Harvey Hansen who snapped the two pictures of Leslie Carroll, and Wallace Kirkland who has captured for all time the appeal of the injured fawn, Calamity Jack.

CHAPTER SIX

The photographs are by Rue; the quotes are from the King James version of the Bible.

* * *

Finally I wish to pay an overdue tribute to my wife Gladys who has helped me with all my books, poetry and other writing since we first met in our mid-teens. She mothered our two bright children, and reads the endless drafts of my manuscripts, making wise suggestions. She also tolerates the variations in mood which seem to be part of my creative process.

Sterling North